Silence, Ecstasy, Happiness

How I Learned to Meditate as a Monk and Discovered Spiritual Tantra

Armin Heining

Cover image: Adobe Stock - City parish church of St. Jacob in Cham/Upper Palatinate
Cover editing: Marko Bussmann

Published in German: May 2020
Translation: Nicholas Elliott, Berlin, Germany
Proofreading: Frank Malensek, Berlin, Germany

ISBN

Paperback: 978-1-916540-22-4 Armin Heining
Hardcover: 978-1-916540-23-1 Armin Heining
E-Book: 978-1-915919-67-0 Armin Heining

Table of Contents

Dedication...i

Acknowledgements...ii

The Author iv

Introduction...2

Chapter 1: Enthusiasm..7

Chapter 2: Downstream..32

Chapter 3: A Shadow Calls..74

Chapter 4: Enlightenment 118

Chapter 5: In the Abyss 145

Chapter 6: A New Day..191

Chapter 7: Being One...240

Epilogue..277

Dedication

For all people on the path to self-actualization.

Acknowledgements

I sincerely thank my faithful companion, Diella C. Nsende, who has suffered through all the versions with me and whose creative power has contributed enormously to the telling of the story.

Together we have succeeded in working out the best possible telling of my life story, and in so doing, we have been truthful to the facts.

I have changed almost all the names in my story to protect the rights of the individuals mentioned and to treat the memories of the people involved in the events of that time with respect.

The two most important mentors on my journey to self-actualization have agreed to the use of their names:

Lejonidas August - theologian, psychologist and psychotherapist, author, and meditation guide for Christian contemplation and Prayer of the Heart, and

Margot Anand - Psychologist, founder of SkyDancing Tantra, trainer, and bestselling author.

I hope that the individuals mentioned feel very much appreciated. I am grateful that they crossed my life, and some are still at my side.

Gerda Alexander introduced me to physical self-awareness

through her book: Eutonie - Ein Weg, published in 1976 (Munich: Kösel), which gave me valuable support in approaching my body from within.

Emmanuel Jungclaussen's 1984 book Aufrichtige Erzählungen eines russischen Pilgers (Freiburg: Herder) was an important companion for me.

I quote Dietrich Bonhoeffer's poem "Von guten Mächten" after the musical version by Siegfried Fietz.

I encountered Gitta Mallasz in her book published in 1984, The Answer of the Angels (Zurich: Daimon).

All Bible passages refer to the Good News Translation.

The first Tantra book I ever held in my hands was by Nick Douglas and Penny Slinger, published in 1986, Das große Buch des Tantra. Sexuelle Geheimnisse und Alchemie der Ekstase (Basel: Sphinx).

The Author

Born in 1960, Armin Heining grew up in the small town of Cham/Upper Palatinate. After graduating from high school, he entered the Benedictine Monastery in Metten/Lower Bavaria and studied Catholic theology at the University of Würzburg.

After years of deep inner conflict and therapeutic processes, in 1990, he left the abbey by mutual agreement.

Following his heart, he founded GAY-TANTRA in Nuremberg in 1992 and became the author and director of numerous bestselling educational films. Heining lives today as an ›urban monk‹ in Berlin. As an international coach, he travels the world teaching his philosophy of happiness: »Meditation is the most intimate way to be with oneself, and the tantric union is the most intimate way to be with another person.«

www.armin-heining.com

info@armin-heining.com

Introduction

»Wow! The breadth and intensity of your experiences are just incredible!«

Never had I seen the American yogi so enthusiastic during my workshops. Until then, I only knew the dignified man with the rugged face and wild curls as quietly reticent. Now this exuberance.

»How do you pass on your insights? What do you offer people who want to learn more?« he asks me.

Is it not obvious? After all, he is taking part in the workshop I am giving.

»Well, I give my courses and, in so doing, hope that the participants take something with them on their journey, that they recognize their own way forward.«

I hesitate.

»I have also produced many educational videos over the years, and there are numerous interviews that deal more with my background.«

The answer is not satisfactory.

»But you can't flip through it, backwards and forwards, make doodles and dog-ear the pages, hear them rustle, or take it from the shelf and give it away, can you?«

»No, I guess not,« I reply reluctantly. The forcefulness with which Santosh speaks to me, the vastness of the desert landscape, which encourages me to think in completely new ways... All at once, new worlds open up inside me.

»Well, for many years, I've been keeping a diary where I record and draw my emotional worlds, ideas, and impressions. I also write down my dreams, of course. They're often filled with important messages!«

»But your story is not only your dreams, no matter how powerful they are,« Santosh points out.

»There's so much more to say. You were not spared anything.«

He is right, of course. When I think back to those years when I had such terrible difficulties with my life, between the age of twenty-five and twenty-seven. I documented everything in my diary in the desperate hope of somehow freeing myself from the enormous psychological pressure. When I write now, it no longer burdens my soul and thoughts. The paper carries the burden of my worries. Such is the ambitious idea behind it, at least.

»You managed to regain your strength. You were able to look back as often as you wanted on what you had achieved in other situations. How far you had already come. Or remind yourself what you already knew. You know...«

He pauses for a moment and looks up at the starry sky.

»By engaging with them, you bring your moments of happiness back to the present. At some point, you start seeing the world differently, for example, no longer experiencing rejection but seizing an opportunity in the same moment, not believing in a final destination but in the possibility of a new path that now lies ahead of you because the old one has ended. The situation around your deacon ordination is a great example of what I mean by this ›mental courage,‹ if I may call it that. It gave you a whole new perspective on your life. Now ask yourself this question: Would you have made it this far on your journey without your diary, without the pages containing all your experiences that you were able to fall back on?«

The penetrating look and the benevolent words touch me deep in my heart. Is there not some truth in that? He is not wrong. I eagerly await his next words.

»Don't you want to make this library available to others, perhaps like you in those years, who believe they've lost control of their lives? Who wants more in their lives than to just ›keep it up?‹ Who no longer believes they can achieve their dreams?«

»You really think so?« I say. I still have some doubts, although the idea of a publication does sound interesting. Maybe the description of my life's journey could really help other people to see their own path more clearly and could help to direct their inner compass.

»Yes, of course, I mean it.« Santosh laughs. As if there were nothing more natural than for him to recommend my next big project to me - late at night in the Californian desert.

»That's where the excitement, the narrative value, and also the educational value lies: In how the tortuous paths finally lead to their destination. Even when the last glimmer of hope seems to be extinguished. Even on a seemingly dark night. A new day dawns, and with it, the light of a new day illuminates your way. And gives you courage. And gives you the strength to go on.«

»Yes!«

From the bottom of my heart, I agree with him. I must agree with him. That is the way it was for me. At the same time, I cannot ignore the downside.

»But it will take time. And how many times have I asked myself: ›When will it end?‹« I say.

»Of course, it takes time, Armin. Everything in life takes time. But what I find so encouraging about your story is that it shows that it's worth it to go a long way, with all its forks, apparent dead ends, and constant switchbacks. Even if it takes a long time and is exhausting, and history seems to repeat itself. Even in circles, things go on!«

How many times in the past months have I thought back to this nocturnal conversation around the merrily flickering campfire when the writing of the book only proceeded at a crawling pace, the multitude of discarded manuscripts straining my patience. Year after year, I waited for the right inspiration to bring me further: to tell lively and vividly what happened to me, to describe the surprising turns that gave my life new direction and unexpected momentum.

My story is not about you and me or about leaders and persons but about the greater plan that appears behind all our encounters, however, they may be arranged.

Chapter 1: Enthusiasm

I never opened up the way I did with Ulrich, Brother Ulrich, actually. But our intimate conversations – in his modest cell or during our long walks – make me forget that I am talking to a monk.

Somehow the words just come to me, and it seems the most natural thing in the world to simply say them. Merely wanting to express what drives me, stops me, holds me, or blocks me, brings me to a standstill, and makes me freeze. Maybe I will be able to cope with my life if I can finally tell someone what really happens to me.

»I would rather confide in my parish priest, Fr. Ellinger, than my father,« I say strongly.

I cannot imagine telling him about Arnulf and the recurring nightmare that has haunted me for so many years. I do not want to imagine how my strict father would react if he knew everything.

»Reverend Ellinger listens to me and doesn't judge. He seems really modern and open,« I conclude thoughtfully. »And he accepts me for who I am. I do not have to justify myself,« I say quickly, hoping to be honest without saying too much.

»Isn't that what a real priest is supposed to do?« Brother Ulrich says, looking at me seriously.

»Absolutely. I've always liked how empathetic and gentle priests are. I think that impressed me from the very beginning. That is definitely a reason why I would like to be a priest myself. They are generally respected, and they are the center of attention during the service. Furthermore, the people who live in our town respect the assistant pastor and pastor. I feel like there is just something special about them.«

»I completely understand what you want to say: clergymen stand out from society and get to enjoy special recognition – through their social position«, Ulrich says.

»Like you, I often felt more accepted in church than in my own home.« He is speaking my mind.

»My mother is vigorous in command at home; my father stays quietly in the background. There is a lot of tension.«

»My house is rather high-tension all the time,« I counter.

»That bad?«

»Yes!« I confirm energetically and add frankly: »My father is really hot-tempered and authoritarian, even though he is friendly on the outside.«

I take a deep breath.

»He helps friends with their tax returns, and he is always there for them in case of problems. He knows all about taxes and authorities because he works for the urban department of finances. But at home, he is usually in a bad mood around us.«

Ulrich appears troubled.

»Really. I feel that my father simply passed on to me the pressure and constraints he experienced in his childhood. At home, I have to put on a performance, even if it contradicts how I feel.«

»Care to share an example?«

»Every Saturday before lunch, he shouts: ›Armin! Shoeshine!‹«

I imitate Father's stern tone.

»Even now?«

»Even now. Even though I am sixteen years old now and doing other things.«

Talking about this Saturday ritual with a stranger not only makes me aware of how absurd it is but also reminds me how hopeless I feel: »Refusing is pointless. My father won't stand for it.«

»Oh, my mother is the same way,« Ulrich nods. »Compromises are completely foreign to her. Her will is the law.«

»Before, it used to be even worse than now. He would wait impatiently for me on the stairs outside our house. I had to rush to get all the family's shoes out of the kitchen and put them neatly outside the door. We cleaned the dirt off every single shoe meticulously with our brushes. Even when cleaning, he commented on everything and never let me out of his sight, not even for a moment. ›Don't make a fuss!‹ he would snarl at me harshly when I worked slowly. When I didn't work fast enough, he would shout: ›Go on, don't give me a hard time!‹«

Encouraged by the parallels in our family histories, I became more open.

»If I still didn't do it his way, he would throw the dirty brush at me. The second step was to carefully grease the shoes and then polish them until they shone. But then he would say, ›You can do that on your own!‹. And so on Saturdays, I would sit outside our front door and polish shoes while my friends ran around and had fun.«

»That is humiliating. Especially in front of your friends.«

Yes, that is exactly how these Saturdays feel: humiliating. Although we hardly know each other, Ulrich says exactly what is on my mind.

»The worst comes at the end. When I was done, my father carefully examined all the polished shoes. This is the part I was most afraid of: if they were not shiny, he would beat me – in front of everyone else. Then I was ashamed and had to cry. And because I cried, he locked me in the bathroom.«

»Oh my. What a terrible experience!«

Ulrich's obvious dismay makes it even clearer to me how

little support I get at home.

»And I imagine there is no use talking to your father either, is there? Those who are authoritarian always think they are right. Isn't that true?«

I nod silently. He sums up my family's circumstances with remarkable astuteness.

»Unfortunately, in many families, it is the same way: parents see things differently from their children and defend their point of view no matter what. There is no point in protesting.«

Is he describing his own life? It sounds very similar to mine.

»Sometimes I just feel burned out and completely alone in a losing race.«

»I know what you mean. But what about your older brother? Does he stand up for you?«

»No, not really. I have siblings, but I am lonely. My sister is ten years younger. My brother is three years older and wants to do things on his own. He has completely different interests than me. He would rather spend time with our sister or his girlfriend than with me. Besides, he is much better in school. We do not really have much in common.«

»Is your mother nice? How do you get along with her?«

Good question. My mother is a very unique case; I like to think.

»Better than with my father, I guess.«

I pause. »She puts me back together, more or less, when I feel withdrawn and powerless.«

I take a deep breath.

»But if she is having a migraine, I can not depend on her anymore. Then she needs absolute rest and only wants to be alone. And I'm literally all alone and without anyone on my side like she doesn't even exist.«

»That is certainly hard.« Brother Ulrich nods.

Because he is a good listener, I feel compelled to tell him more.

»My mother actually chased me once with a kitchen spoon!«

»What? Really?«

He looks at me in disbelief.

»Believe it or not: One day, I was playing with my friends by a stream near our house after school. Suddenly there was nothing more important than climbing up the wall that rose up beside the bank. Of course, we did not notice how late it had become. But my mother did; she had her eye on the clock the whole time. Out of the blue, she was standing at the top of the wall with a wooden spoon in her hand and screaming: ›Lunch's been ready for hours! I'm waiting for you, and you're fooling around! I was scared and worried – and what are you doing?‹ I was embarrassed, of course, to be scolded like that in front of my friends. I wanted to apologize. But she didn't listen at all; she waved the wooden spoon as if she wanted to hit me. Then she chased me – with the spoon raised – all the way home as if I were a cow on my way back to the barn. Later, as she lay down on the sofa, I found out that she was having a bad migraine again. She wanted to rest, but instead, she had to run after me because I was thinking only about myself again. She expected more thoughtfulness from me, she told me.«

»Oh, that sounds familiar. That sounds just like my mother's strict temperament. I also suffered a lot from her moods. She was always very quick to criticize and blame. I never seemed to deserve her approval or praise.«

Lost in thought, his gaze wanders off into the distance.

»Exactly!« I cry out.

»Sometimes I wonder what my parents even think of me. I feel like I am never enough for them. I often make my mother worry about me, and I'm always afraid that my father wants to drive the happiness out of me.«

Tears come to my eyes at the thought of not being loved by my father as I am.

»Do you think it is possible that your parents still see the good in you?« he asks quietly.

»I can hardly imagine,« I said soberly.

Only the ringing of the bell tears me out of the silence in which we had been sitting for several minutes, a silence that often accompanies my conversations with Ulrich. On the other hand, I am becoming more comfortable with the bell calling me seven times a day to our service and prayer.

›To our service.‹ As if I were already one of them. I am here just to visit the Metten Monastery in Lower Bavaria. A six-day trial, and then we will see.

»Why are you visiting our monastery during your Christmas holidays?« was one of Ulrich's first questions.

»I have wished for a long time to get away from the boredom at home and have a different kind of Christmas,« I say with surprising honesty.

»I really want to spend more time in the presence of God and to seek dialogue with Him in prayer. During the two-week Christmas holiday, I would like to have more time for silent devotion and to get away from the world. My parents have other plans for the family. And their plans do not fit mine.«

»Hm.« Ulrich nods thoughtfully.

»I can understand that. When there is no one around to share your desire to be near God, it makes you lonely.«

I could not have put it better myself.

»That's right. It's just that nobody in my family understands that. At least I am lucky with my confessor: I can confide in him without hesitation; he always knows what to do and ...«

»... and he told you about the monastery,« Ulrich says, summing up my story in a nutshell.

»He did. Because I told him I was looking for a community where I was not the only one who wanted to be closer to God. Church visits are too few, too short, too fleeting; they are only skin-deep.«

»Why did you choose us? There are several other monasteries in the area: Schweickelberg, Niederalteich, Plankstetten, Beuron, Weltenburg.«

»I guess it's just practical; Metten is the closest«, I reply dryly. We look at each other, and both have to laugh.

»I would say that your practical mind has led you in the right direction: the Benedictine order is committed to prayer but also attentive to the world – in contrast to the strict, contemplative religious communities.«

»I like the balance. It is also reflected in your motto, the Benedictine motto: ›Ora et labora.‹«

»Our service is to praise God. The work of the monks is prayer; even when we eat, it is worship.«

With a reverence that I have seldom experienced in myself, I reply: »You are not too radical; the pendulum does not swing too far in any direction. I also seek the right measure, this inner balance, for myself.«

»Time will tell,« Ulrich answers with a friendly smile.

»You are still young; you will be fine.«

I am too young – only sixteen– to be allowed to make a formal decision right now. I must first get my high school diploma, then I can ask for admission into the monastery. Nevertheless, my ›monastery vacation‹ affects me strongly.

At home in Cham, I even get up early for my standards to attend the early mass before school, a very important routine. But here, the day begins at four forty. That takes getting used to. I am not really awake yet when I speak the first prayer together with the monks.

Prayers indeed – in the morning, at noon, and in the evening, along with songs to give thanks after lunch and dinner. Each time a different hymnbook: a thick one in the morning and evening, a thin one at noon. The language changes too: midday prayer in German, the others in Latin. That is confusing. But I have Ulrich at my side, who patiently tells me what to do.

My arrival was like a jump in cold water because the evening prayer was coming up, and I had no idea what to do. Monastic rituals have little in common with the service in my city parish church.

»How will I find my way around? I don't want to do anything wrong.« I did not want to mess up the routine or anything.

»Just follow me and do what I do. You will be in the last seat on edge of the choir stalls. We will start by singing four Latin psalms,« Ulrich replied reassuringly.

Latin too! If he only knew: It is the subject I despise most.

Ulrich opened the Antiphonale, a thick, leather-bound tome, and showed me the different songs using the colored bookmarks.

»Then we sit down and listen to the Scriptures. Afterwards, we sing the Magnificat again, standing up. It is the solemn climax of the ecclesial evening prayer, the daily recurring hymn praising Mary.«

The corresponding page was marked with a purple ribbon.

At six o'clock on the dot, I stood for the first time with the monks in the half-moon shape of the choir room behind the baroque abbey church's high altar. In contrast to the cold vaulted corridors on the same floor, the apse is heated and comfortably warm. The dark choir stalls with their elaborate carvings form a semicircle with a view of the cantor's artistically carved lectern. Above the foldable seats is a small ledge for to lean against, a noticeable relief for the body after standing for so long. Frater Ulrich showed me the seat reserved for me on the very outside of the row.

At the first stroke of the bell, the organ began to play

softly. From the front, Abbot Berthold's high voice rang out: »In nomine Patris et Filii et Spiritus Sancti.«

With a prolonged »Amen« all the monks answered at once. I sang the evening prayer with them in Latin. I watched the monk next to me very closely to see when I should bow or stand up and sit, stand or kneel.

But I am most impressed by the extraordinary ceremony of the monks leaving the choir to go to the dining room. When they step over the threshold of the choir room, the large, pointed hood, which is part of the Benedictine monks' robes, is pulled up far over their heads. Deeply veiled, they walk in a procession through the baroque cloister to the refectory. Behind them, dressed in civilian clothes, the image of detachment strikes me. Only when they enter the dining room do they remove their hoods again.

When I arrive in the brightly lit room, I stand behind my seat like the other monks. They conceal their folded hands under their black robes, and I lower my head as they do and listen to the abbot's grace. With a loud »Amen« we take our seats.

Symbolic of the monastery's seclusion, the monks once again pull on their hoods after grace has been said. Their gaze remains humbly lowered while the word is recited from the Holy Scriptures.

When the waiters have served the soup and the table reading starts, they take off their hoods again.

Everyone remains devoutly silent and looks at their plate. Only the monk in charge of the table reading speaks. While we eat, he reads first from the Bible and later from a travel book.

These customs have not changed for centuries; At the same time and in the same way, every day, the same thing happens. And in 1976, I was suddenly right in the middle of it, allowed to participate and help keep the tradition alive—side by side with ordained monks, as if I belonged to their community. To have a place here and feel welcome affects me deeply in my heart.

»How do you feel? Can you imagine living here – or in a monastery at all?«

Ulrich and I have just finished a walk around the monastery's impressively spacious grounds. With its workshops, facilities, and power source, it is as well-equipped as a small village.

And the main building is especially impressive in its baroque splendor: lots of gold, angels, and ornamentation. The baroque library is filled with statues larger than life – these alone are quite moving.

There are even public events in the monastery – I did not know that until Ulrich showed me the festival hall: »There are regular concert evenings here. It is very popular as a venue because of the excellent acoustics. Even beyond the borders of Lower Bavaria, this is known by people.«

And they watch TV! With ten red upholstered recliners neatly arranged in two rows, I could hardly believe I was in a monastery. The Metten monastery amazes me again and again.

But is it a place where I could live?

»What I like most of all is the tight daily schedule,« I replied evasively.

Ulrich looks at me sideways in surprise.

»Seriously? This is what most visitors cannot stand. They complain that they don't have enough personal space.«

He snorts contemptuously.

»Well, that's not why we're here,« I affirm.

»We?«

»What?«

»You just said, ›That's not why we're here.‹ Do you already think of yourself as a monk?«

I laugh, embarrassed. I didn't even notice the slip.

»Maybe. I like it here. And I like the clear order of every day. I usually fall into a hole during the holidays, and become moody and inaccessible because I need structure. Here the regular prayer times give me stability. And the community is always there for each other. It feels like a beautiful life.«

»It is a good, meaningful life if we lead it God-fearingly,« Ulrich replies with a seriousness that I had not yet noticed in him.

»And if you really like it that much, maybe it is the right thing for you.«

I lower my head. I'd very much like to belong.

But dare I hope to be accepted here? I mean, it is the Catholic Church, with its strict principles of faith, that decides who may commit themselves to a monastic community for life. Not Ulrich, who might have some sympathy for me. At least for the time being. Who knows how he will react when he knows the whole truth?

The ringing of the monastic bell for evening prayer relieves me of the need to answer. My silence is no longer noticeable. I am absorbed, so to speak, in the monastic silence that covers the monastery corridors like a heavy blanket and seems to nip any noise in the bud. In my diary, I described it as a dead silence. A phenomenon that takes getting used to if you are used to the constant noise of a busy family.

But beyond the silence, there is surprisingly a lot going on behind the monastery walls. Perhaps this is due to how many young monks there are. Until now, I have mostly associated monasticism with old age – starting from about the age of fifty.

Now I notice that many young men live here. Of course, this speaks in favor of Metten: There are a lot of people my same age.

Confident peers. Between evening prayer and monastic silence of the night, they like to meet in the teachers' office of the boarding school attached to the monastery. I have already been there twice at the personal invitation of Father Jeremiah. The fact that such a popular prefect invites me to one of his festive evenings tells me that I am accepted.

Nevertheless, the excitement quickly becomes too much for me. It is too loud, too many people I don't know well, and too much effort to focus. The final few days, I prefer to spend on my own, completing my diary entries or praying. In this case, I head to the boarding school chapel outside the cloister's walls. There are the Christmas holidays, so I can be sure that nobody is going to the small church.

I sit down on a bench and let the uplifting atmosphere take its effect on me: the intense smell of incense, the eternal light in front of the tabernacle, the soothing semi-darkness.

»Dear God, I do not know now whether I should stay here or go off with the others. I feel a burning inside me, like an open wound. I do not know what to do against the pain, this great inner pain. What means more to me? Would I rather be alone with myself in silence because you give me everything?

Or do I care more about the community? Where is my place? Where do I belong?«

»Is everything all right with you?« Ulrich asks me anxiously after breakfast.

How perceptive he is. The other day he noticed immediately that I had retreated into my shell and wanted to stay invisible.

»I am all right,« I mumble.

»Come on, let's go for a walk. The cool air will do you good.«

I join him reluctantly but quickly realize that he is right. The fresh breeze clears my mind. And encourages me to speak openly.

»Sometimes I find it hard to adapt to new situations,« I start hesitantly. When Ulrich does not reply, I just keep talking. His silence is encouraging.

»It has always been the case that I cannot cope with too much stimulation. I don't like to talk about it because I think it makes me look ridiculous. Maybe other people feel disparate. A few people, more or less, what difference does it make? For me, it makes a big contrast. It's been that way since I was a kid. During a ski trip, I had a kind of breakdown because of all the people on the slopes and then the skiing down over and over again, it was too much for me, and I felt overwhelmed. I had a sharp pain in my heart and a burning sensation in my chest as if a wound had opened up. But what hurt me most was that my parents did not care. They took note of the incident but did not question anything or arrange a medical examination. To this day, they still have no idea what to do with my feelings.«

»That is a terrible story.«

That he can always express his sympathy in such simple words and yet still be able to reach me – that really feels good.

»You know, I have never talked to anyone about this before,« I confide in him quietly.

»Really? Then just say it. Maybe it will help you in the future.«

As if it were that simple. But maybe it is a step in the right direction.

»In any case, I figured out that the only time I do not suffer from anxiety is when there seems to be just God and me. Nothing more. Only then am I free from this unbearable inner burning.«

»Then, prayer and attending service is really like a balm for your soul ...«

»... yes, like a band-aid on my inner wound,« I enthusiastically continue the sentence he started. To be understood like this feels like a gift from heaven.

»Staying in the monastery must be like a biotope for you, a

place where you can really flourish – if you refuse Father Jeremiah's invitation now and then.«

Ulrich laughs gently.

»Oh. Did I offend him?« I didn't mean to.

»No, it's all right; he doesn't hold a grudge against you. We all want you to feel comfortable. Jeremiah has no idea that you would rather be by yourself.« I sigh with relief. At least I do not have to worry about that.

»Please do not tell him about this conversation either. I want to keep what I had to say just between us. It is very important to me,« I say so pleadingly that it almost makes me uncomfortable. I am not used to confiding such deep secrets to someone I have known for only a few days. I do not want to seem weak.

»Don't worry, Armin. I'm not a snitch.«

I feel a deep sigh of relief in my chest. Ulrich always finds the right words of support. What a weight has been lifted from my shoulders. I feel liberated and start to see things in a completely different way.

Not even the heavy monastic silence can depress my mood as it was before. All the fears I was able to let go of are gone for now and no longer haunt me in the deathly silence of the monastery corridors. As if a door long closed has opened in my mind, I now feel the imperturbable silence penetrating me and creating a particularly wide and open space for encountering God. Now I am ready to join in the Gregorian chants and the Christmas joy of the psalm prayers. In the hymns of praise and biblical stories, I recognize a mirror for my own feelings: clarified, joyful, and in high spirits by my standards.

Retreating into silence and remaining quiet became of central importance shortly before the end of my visit. Even the daily tasks are reduced to a minimum in order to set the tone for the High Feast of the Epiphany.

By entering into deep silence, we get rid of impure thoughts. We clothe ourselves in robes, humbly preparing ourselves for closeness to God.

At nine o'clock in the morning, the solemn Pontifical Mass begins. I was not aware until then that Abbot Berthold, who holds the rank of the bishop of the monastic community, is also endowed with a bishop's insignia: the mitre on his head, the crosier in his hand, and the cross over his chest. He enters the church from the nave's rear entrance while the organ plays fervently. The monks and priests precede him. I take a seat in the front pew so that I can follow the ceremony up close. The sublime atmosphere not only lifts me up and moves me to tears but also makes me believe there might be a place for me here. This could be the community where I want to belong.

On January 7th, I pack my bag with a heavy heart. One last time I walk with Abbot Berthold, the lively leader of the monastery, to the impressive archway at the end of the cloister. This iron grating separates the inner enclosure of the monastery from the world. Once again, I experience how the abbot opens the gate without a key or visible turning of the knob so that with a loud crack, the heavy door swings to the side.

»I am glad you were here, Armin. It was nice to meet you.«

»Thank you for a very memorable time.«

Abbot Berthold nods kindly and offers me his hand in farewell.

Then the iron door behind me closes in its lock. A slight shiver trickles down my back: My quiet life in the monks' retreat is locked out.

Shortly thereafter, I begin my laborious journey home with the Bockerlbahn train from Deggendorf to Plattling, further on via Regensburg and Schwandorf back to Cham. The several-hour journey gives me enough time to sort out my wandering thoughts. As the snow-covered houses and meadows rush by outside, I think back to how nice it was of Ulrich to give me friendly words to remember. I was sad to have to leave Metten already. The week had passed by in a flash. Was it only six days ago that I visited Brother Ulrich in his monk's cell for the first time?

I can still remember how I absorbed the atmosphere and every detail in order not to forget anything later, preserving these first impressions in my memory, how I walked together with him through the cold vault on the ground floor, up the imposing stone staircase to the first floor of the baroque cloister. Here, a red sisal runner on a white marble floor points the way to the cells of the older monks. Simple small, squat doors with wrought-iron locks and handles, surrounded by marble decorations in delicate pastel pink and fresh white, line the spacious cloister corridor. The path to Ulrich's room leads up a more modern staircase to the second floor. Here a plain brown runner lies on the creaky wooden floor. Only the name plates are as pretty as they are below.

A monk's cell like this contains only the most necessary things: There is a bed and wardrobe, and also a desk and a chair for a visitor. It is cosy, nevertheless. This might have something to do with Ulrich's compassion; it fills the room.

»Did you like it here, Armin?«

»I haven't felt this good in a long time. I feel a connection with myself, and I am at peace with God. I am happy that I got to know you all and made new connections. Seldom have I felt so at home as I do here, as if I belonged here. Unlike in my family.«

»The monastic community is a completely different way of life than that of a family,« Ulrich said, giving me something to think about.

»More than anything, it's a way of living together that might suit me.«

And I confided in him a thought that was still completely new to me: »To be honest, I could never have imagined starting my own family, with a wife, children, and everything. I do not think I want to live like that.«

The tranquility of the monastic silence gives me completely new insights and opens up unimagined perspectives.

»It is quite possible. Perhaps you are born to be a monk,« he said seriously.

»You know what?« I said, taking up the thread of the conversation after a while.

»Tell me,« he said with a little smile.

»I don't feel as strange as I used to, but like everything is now in the right place.«

»I hope for your sake that it stays that way at home.«

Ulrich's smile is heartwarming.

A very wishful thinking. Because I know it will be different. I know the long shadow that hangs over my life and can easily overcome the many kilometers that lie between my hometown and the prospect of a new life. Deliberately, Ulrich did not find out about this. Because I did not want to admit how I really was, for this reason, of course, I never mentioned the name ›Arnulf‹, although my thoughts regularly revolve around him.

Arnulf is just as bad at school as I am, in the same Catholic student youth group as I am, and faithful and sensitive as I am. In many ways, I feel attracted to him and attracted by him. I enjoy being close to him, embracing him, and praying with him. With him, I experienced closeness for the first time. And, of course, I hope he feels the same as I do – in every respect.

How to reconcile my preference for boys with my deep faith I cannot answer myself. Is that the reason why my nightmares revolve around this fear exactly? »Either I'll become a saint, or I'll end up in the gutter, homeless and under a bridge.« There seems to be no way out, and I always wake up bathed in sweat.

How can I reconcile my desire for closeness to God with my vivid fantasies without being an outcast? For me, sexuality is bad. And homosexuality is doubly bad. Being attracted to other boys, being a homosexual, is unimaginable in this world as I know it. If I follow my desires, I will never become anything – of that, I am sure. For a moment, I wonder how many exclamation marks I have written in my diary next to the date. Each one marks a day when I lost control again, ejaculated, and felt ashamed.

I will never forget my father's disgusted expression when he once spoke about a man ›from the other bank‹ who had lived alone at the edge of the village – »and suddenly, under Hitler, he was gone,« he remembered. My father finds the very thought of homosexuality disgusting. Am I supposed to expect him to understand?

No wonder I tried to escape from his narrow-mindedness even as a child and spend as much time as possible away from home. As if I were a ›village broom‹, my father criticized me disapprovingly when I returned to the village full of curiosity and with the urge for freedom. Light, sun, water, and fresh air were already the elements that made me blossom and feel the irrepressible joy of life.

But life will not always be so simple. I will not always be able to run away. At the latest, when I graduate from high school, the seriousness of life will have to meet my deepest fears. How can I live a life that feels real? How can homosexuality be combined with my desire for a life in harmony with God?

Chapter 2: Downstream

As soon as it can be arranged, I find myself in Reverend Ellinger's rustic parish house cozy parsonage. He has been counseling me for some time and is always happy to hear how I am doing. On the way to his office today, I noticed the creaking of the old wooden floorboards.

»That's the monastic creak,« I recognize happily. The thought of Metten refuses to let go of me.

»In the name of the Father, and of the Son, and of the Holy Spirit.«

»Amen,« I reply. This ritual precedes our every conversation, no matter how personal it is.

»How was it?«

I do not answer right away. Over time I have learned that first, the pipe must be lit. Only then can Father Ellinger listen calmly.

»What have you got to report, Armin?«

»I don't even know where to begin.«

My head is still spinning from the wealth of new impressions.

»Well, the solitude is very particular. I think it's what impressed me the most. It's what's stuck with me the most, in a way. This keeping to oneself in the cloister, really living apart from the world, was a completely new experience. And the seclusion is permanent, not over at the end of the service like it is here. When I step out of the church here in Cham, I'm immediately back in the world. In my world and, therefore, in my family. With my parents and everything.

»In the monastery, there is a gate that locks out everything worldly. A beautiful gate, by the way, wrought iron with floral vines. When I first stepped through it, I not only entered the enclosure, but I also literally turned my back on the world as I knew it. This gave me a chance to participate in a completely different life and to be different from who I am here.«

»In what way? What do you mean?«

»I felt appreciated there. They looked at me differently; I was no longer the oddball or eternal outsider. In the monastery, I met like-minded people; we were united in faith. The Armin, whom no one understands, was basically left outside the gate. And you know what's best?«

My mind is racing. One thought is barely finished before I describe the next: »They are so young!«

»They? Who do you mean?«

Father Ellinger was obviously having trouble following my jumps.

»The other monks that I spent most of my time with.

They're not so much older than me. Do you remember before when I said, ›I hope they're not that old at Metten?‹«

»Yes, I remember that very well. You were quite worried about that.«

»And it was completely unfounded. We were on the same wavelength.«

Now I am really getting into it.

»I got on particularly well with Father Ulrich. He's in his mid-twenties, studies Catholic theology in Salzburg, and will soon take his solemn vows. He looked out for me during my stay. We spent a lot of time together.«

I notice that I am getting almost rapturous, thinking about how much those conversations have helped me.

»That was ... special. I don't really know anymore why we got along so well, but I knew right away I could trust him. And that was the right choice. After I had the courage to talk about how I'm always unhappy and tell him about my ›inner wound‹, I felt free. He understood me and said it was okay if I didn't always participate in the spontaneous get-togethers with the other young monks because it was simply too much for me ... oh, I didn't mention that yet. In the evenings, we met ...«

»Armin?«

»Yes, Father Ellinger?«

»You were talking about the ›inner wound‹ and the

problems it causes you.«

Oh, right; I guess I got carried away. I was too excited and had not noticed.

»Right! The weird ›inner burning‹.«

I have to take a moment to pull myself together and find my thoughts again.

»With Ulrich, I could talk about what it's like to constantly feel defeated and like I need to escape. Only in silence and prayer, in dialogue with God, do I feel truly safe. And he understood that. He said that worship and prayer were a ›balm for my soul‹. That's why living in a monastery could be the right place for me. Actually, Ulrich said, the monastery could be like a ›Biotope‹ to me.«

I quickly correct myself to be as accurate as possible.

»And is that true?« says Reverend Ellinger through thick cloud of aromatic pipe smoke.

»Would you consider visiting another monastery? After all, it seems this has been quite a positive experience, and you describe it very vividly.«

»It was positive the whole time. The strict rhythm of the monastic day is just what I need.«

»Oh, getting up early didn't bother you?«

Father Ellinger sounds more than surprised.

»Perhaps I should say: it took some getting used to. But then it was fine. What was more important to me was the feeling of being held together, as if by a net, through whose strands I cannot fall because one event follows the next so closely. That really helped me to concentrate and reflect on the essentials. The bigger this tight net stretches, the more hours of the day it contains, the better. Do you know what I mean?«

Am I making sense? My head is still spinning.

»Have you already thought of doing this again and getting to know another monastic community, another monastery?«

That does not sound bad. My thoughts are not this far along, however. I am still in the process of sorting out my experiences; I am trying to form a completely new picture of my life.

Moreover, the six days in Metten were something so exceptional it had never occurred to me that I could do it again. Is this once-in-a-lifetime experience repeatable?

»You could then find out what other monastic communities have to offer you. Perhaps they will complement your experience.«

Doubt is written all over my face, so Father Ellinger continues.

»And you would have that structure in your vacation time that you miss outside of school. As you said yourself: ›Outer structure creates inner order.«

I am nodding. He's right, of course. There is nothing I miss more over the holidays than a fixed daily schedule.

»How are things at home? Has anything changed after your visit? Maybe you brought a whole new perspective with you from the monastery?«

A new perspective on my parents, my home? Not at all. I shake my head, deflecting.

»I may have been greatly influenced by the six days of my visit. But my parents are still the same; they haven't changed, not in the least. What I do remains foreign to them. I am still a stranger to them. That's why it's no use telling them about my unforgettable experience. They didn't even pick me up from the station.«

I still feel the bitterness of standing alone on the platform and not being able to tell anyone about the incredible days at the monastery as soon as I arrived.

»My father still thinks visiting a monastery is a crazy idea, so I don't know how he would react if I visited another one. And my mother stays out of it. Which is equivalent to a lack of support.«

Once again, I feel a knot loosening inside me as I formulate the obvious in the presence of Father Ellinger: »This, for example, is a big difference from my stay in the monastery. I felt accepted by the community immediately, even though they didn't know me. They gave me the feeling that I was one of them. Whereas with my parents, it's like they don't know what to think of me. I am a stranger to them. What I feel, what I do – it's not part of their world. I don't think they can put themselves in my place.«

»But in the monastery, you were allowed to be you.«

»Absolutely! After I was able to tell Ulrich how I felt and I had the impression that he took me seriously, the whole atmosphere was suddenly transformed. The deep, impenetrable silence, which lay over the processions through the corridors, for example, suddenly no longer repelled me but welcomed me instead. And then I felt ready for them. Suddenly my soul unfolded in an unexpected way and climbed to the highest heights. That's impossible here.«

I pause. I hope he has not misunderstood me.

»It's nothing against you, of course,« I explain, embarrassed. »I didn't mean it that way. You support me as much as possible and give me space. The whole environment is just different here.«

Father Ellinger does not seem to have taken it the wrong way. Quite the contrary: he understands me.

»That's not how I understood you, either. You simply learned the meaning of sacred silence. In a monastery, it's very special; it gives divine insight.«

»That's certainly true. In the silence there, God feels much closer. To experience that again, to immerse myself in the silence one more time, to receive God's word – that would really be something.«

The idea of a next visit to a monastery is becoming clearer in my mind. As if I had never been away, I picture myself in the company of young monks having a snack in the refectory or praising God together in song and prayer.

»Well, now that you've given it a try, just let your curiosity guide you.«

I nod. This is advice I intend to heed.

The value of this conversation, in which I was able to summarize, together with my confessor, the recent changes in my state of mind, becomes clear quite quickly: the tension at home was easier to bear since I started to look forward to the prospect of further visits to the monastery during the next holidays.

So much has been going through my mind in the last weeks. Suddenly I can take chances more easily because I see things differently. It feels as if blockades in my head have been removed, and a path has been created for a new way of thinking. I even started to like going to school when I realized that a clever combination of my favorite subjects can finally help me get good grades for my last high school years.

I certainly will not graduate if I take Latin and Math. I enjoy Latin conjugation and declination about as much as I like algebra and mathematical theorems.

Instead, in my senior year, playing in the school orchestra became my main focus. Not only is it a lot of fun, but it is also an easy way to get a lot of credits.

My extracurricular involvement in the Catholic Students Youth Group also proves to be a distinct stroke of luck. I get to know Adrian and Arnd, who go to the Humanities high school next door and are the same year as me.

At first, our common ground is the weekly meeting of the CSY group. In a short time, they became my closest friends. I find them to be sensitive, thoughtful, and prudent.

Even my parents consider them to be ›good company‹ because they come from good families and their parents have respectable professions, as my father notes with approval.

With them, I experienced the bonds of friendship that I had longed for growing up. Neither of them has a girlfriend. And nobody knows that one of us is gay. For me, there is no reason to open up and reveal my sexual orientation or to provoke questions that nobody seems to ask.

As time flies by, I find myself at a crossroads before I know it: the last year of school has begun, and I am expected to make a decision that will determine the rest of my life: »After graduating from high school, the serious side of life begins,« my father likes to say with a threatening expression. Like every time when I am not sure what to do, I hope that Father Ellinger will give me direction.

On a gloomy day in November 1979, I wait patiently for the first puffs of smoke to drift through the office before I present the purpose of my visit: concern for my future.

»I should finally start thinking about what will happen after graduation. I expect the draft notice every day. By the time it arrives, at the latest, I'll have to make a decision.«

»Hm.«

More little clouds rise and spread the special smell of pipe smoke, which I have come to associate with mental clarification.

He puffs deeply several times before he asks thoughtfully: »What do you have in mind?«

»Well, I'm thinking about joining a monastery after graduation. But I'm still not sure. I met the Brothers of Mercy. Despite my father's objections, I spent time with the Jesuits and the Capuchin monks. I've already told you how important it was for me to follow my heart, to do what I feel passionate about.«

I see Reverend Ellinger nodding. And then I realize what

he already seems to know: »You know what? Actually, Metten is the only one I'm interested in,« I say in a firm voice, bold from my revelation.

»Oh, yes? I still remember the conversation we had right after your visit there.«

»Right. Out of all the monasteries, I had the most profound experience at Metten.«

»And yet you doubt.«

Though my confessor sounds matter-of-fact, I can hear the concern resonating in his voice.

»I'm supposed to make a decision now and forever. That frightens me,« I say, trying to explain what has been bothering me for some time.

Father Ellinger draws deeply on his pipe before answering.

»I'll give you a suggestion: Make a pro and contra lists on two sheets of paper. On one sheet, you write Pros and Cons Military Service, and on the other, Pros and Cons Monastery. You will then be able to tell which future you're more attracted to.«

I like the suggestion; it sounds quite helpful.

»I am sure you'll come to a ›discernment of spirits‹ this way.«

»Come to a what?« I have never heard of this term before.

»If you follow my advice, it will be revealed whether God has ordained you for the monastic life. Beloved, do not believe every spirit but test the spirits to see whether they are from God... (John 1, chapter 4, verse 1). Therefore: examine carefully the influences to which you are exposed. Judge and learn to discern which spirit they come from. Examine them according to the standards of reason on the basis of the Holy Scripture and the knowledge of great church scholars and saints. Consider also the fruits of the tree, as in the Gospel of Matthew, chapter 7, verse 17: ...every healthy tree bears good fruit.. . With this spirit in mind, create the two lists. Allow yourself the time to pray on them. Move the individual arguments inwards and be sure, Armin, the Spirit of God will show itself in your decision.«

As soon as I arrive home, I prepare my decision-making tool on two large sheets of paper by writing down all the arguments I can think of. For several weeks I reflected on them in an inner dialogue and internalized them in my prayers before finally coming to a decision in April 1980: to pursue the deep and unforgettable experience I had during my monastic vacation at the Metten Abbey.

Then everything happens very quickly. I inform Abbot Berthold of my decision in a letter asking for admission to the monastery. His answer comes surprisingly quickly, and I am happy. Before accepting my application, he wants to meet my parents.

Because the abbot of my future monastery will soon be sitting in our living room, I casually tell my parents at dinner that my plans for the future are now fixed.

»Oh, by the way: Abbot Berthold will come by in two weeks. He wants to talk to you before I enter his monastery in August.«

My father's fork nearly falls out of his hand, my mother is frozen like a pillar of salt, and my sister is speechless.

With a scarlet face, he starts panting.

»Get out!« he tells my sister.

»And you …« His trembling index finger points directly at me, »you really want to join this old men's club? Why am I only finding out about this now?«

His questions are rhetorical, of course. My parents have never been open to discussing my true interests. There is no stopping him now: »…not invested in everything?! It was plenty of money – and for what? So he can go to the monastery afterwards! But that's the youth today. Thinking only of themselves. Only concerned with self-fulfillment! I wish I'd been allowed to get away with it.«

He storms out of the room. »No good deed goes unpunished,« He rants from the next room. I look at my mother, who is still in shock.

»Do you really want to leave us forever?« she asks in a voice choked with tears.

I am not prepared myself for this. To imagine leaving my mother forever? This part had never even occurred to me. My heart starts beating faster.

In the hope of sounding braver than I feel, after a few moments of shock, I reply, »But we'll see each other from time to time.«

Instead of an answer, she silently clears away the sad remains of our meal.

»And how is that supposed to work?« my father bellows out from behind me

»Now, what work ?« I ask irritably and turn to face him.

»This monk in my house. He wants to come here. You just said so.«

He is still trembling with rage.

»He'll call to arrange a visit.« I say, looking my father in the eye. I do not want to be intimidated by his whims anymore. There's no point in openly fighting; I know that. But I can express my views in other ways.

So it arrives that the abbot is sitting in our house a short time later. The mood is complex. Abbot Berthold looks as friendly and kind as I remember him from Metten. The expression on my mother's face is impenetrable. Next to her on the sofa sits my father, who looks like a judge presiding over the court in his living room. Father Wunibald is also here. He chauffeured the abbot to our house today and sits in the second-best armchair.

Abbot Berthold kindly opens the conversation: »What do you think of Armin's decision to enter our monastery?«

Even now, my father does not mince his words. »Armin's often stubborn and rebellious and has not learned to listen to me. I don't believe he will be obedient in a monastery!«

I have known my father's direct approach for years, but these harsh words hit me like a blow. A scrutinizing look at my mother gives me the certainty that I can expect no support from her. An uncomfortable silence spreads through the room.

How will the abbot react?

Confident. As if he could master any kind of situation, he finds a Solomonic answer: »The Rule of the Order explicitly provides for a test period. Three months of candidature are followed by a one-year novitiate and three years of temporary vows. During these periods, not only the monastic community examines the suitability of the candidate. More than that, we trust that during this period, he will reflect consistently on his life with us and will see for himself whether he's willing and able to live in humility according to the Rule of Saint Benedict«

I can hardly imagine it: Leaving in the middle, during the candidacy or the novitiate? Technically, that might be an option. At the same time, simply deciding to leave the monastery feels wrong. I have made my decision in the knowledge that I will bind myself to this monastic community for life, to be its monk forever. This is a promise to myself, and I do not intend to break it.

As I lie in bed at night, I wonder what made my mother finally say what I had longed to hear: »I hope you'll be happy at the monastery.«

She was so moved she even embraced me.

My father also seemed rather impressed when Abbot Berthold and Father Wunibald said goodbye to us after less than an hour. Has he finally realized that his son knows what he is doing and is not simply being foolish? Should I hope that my father will now respect my decisions?

With my final exams steadily approaching, I prepare myself thoroughly for the core exams in geography, history, and chemistry.

A major incentive to get good grades is the trip we have planned following our tests. From the end of May until graduation day at the end of June in 1980, my friends and I wanted to feel as free as possible before the serious side of life began. Essentially, the plan is to let ourselves drift with camping equipment, a borrowed car, and not much money. We plan to call home from the road to see if each of us has passed. If luck is on our side, we will not have to turn back and face a follow-up round of oral exams.

There is only one sure thing on our itinerary: The Catholic Day in West Berlin. Furthermore, Brother Ulrich wrote me that he and other brothers would be there at an information stand representing Metten Abbey – another good reason to go there.

An overwhelming atmosphere awaits us on the western side of the city. Berlin is divided by a wall, but the spirit of freedom and unity that dominates the entire church day seems to have the power to bring down walls, at least in our minds. I experience so much diversity and awakening at the individual events, from controversial, passionate panel discussions and rousing concerts to the genuinely lively church services: it seems as if a fresh, modern wind is giving the Catholic Church new energy. The high number of visitors illustrates this quite clearly. Almost every event is overcrowded. Everyone appears to feel the new spirit of the times. I am no exception. I want to attend everything and to lose myself in the sense of community – which reminds me of the feeling that until now I have only experienced at Metten: to be welcomed exactly as I am. Even with the emotional pain of my ›inner wound‹.

Miraculously, despite all the hustle and bustle, I do not suffer at all inside Berlin. It feels like a good sign. Surely it means that my soul has arrived and is in harmony with the surrounding environment, that I am no longer overwhelmed by the outside world and feel safe, at peace with myself, at an event of the Catholic Church, in the Catholic Church.

If I can already sense what it is like to feel accepted, isn't it time to go one step further and dare to be even more open?

In the course of deciding my professional future, I have succeeded surprisingly well in ignoring what is probably the biggest disruptive factor: my homosexuality.

I am still a few weeks away from entering the monastery, and now I want to know where I stand and who I will be as a monk. Also, the Catholic Day motto, ›Christ's love is stronger‹, seems to me a call to go one step further because Christ's love is stronger than the fear of change or rejection.

And Ulrich will surely be on my side when I open up. That alone makes me feel safe. I have always been able to trust him.

From a distance, I see Ulrich talking to two young men. He seems engaged and warm-hearted, just as I remember him. It means a lot to me that we have kept in touch over the years and that I can turn to him again today.

After ending their conversation, it seems to me a good time for a frank discussion. Until it is my turn, I flip through the attractively designed brochure which describes monastic life in Metten. In the front matter, I see that it was designed by the young Metten community brothers under the direction of Father Jeremias. In my thoughts, I am already wandering with these young monks in black robes over the monastery grounds.

»Hello, Armin.«

I look up in surprise. In my daydream, I had missed the end of his conversation.

»Shall we sit down on the grass over there? I need a moment to catch my breath.«

»Yeah, sure. I was hoping you might have a second for me.«

On the large lawn in front of the Reichstag, Ulrich and I find a nice spot next to three young men who appear to be meditating. Here, it seems anything is possible.

Encouraged by this thought, I immediately ask the question that could change my life: »Is it possible to be a monk and live in a monastery if I am homosexual?«

Ulrich's face does not change. If my direct question surprised him, he did not let it show. »You will not live sexuality. We take the vow of chastity. Therefore, sexual orientation is of no importance.«

His credo sounds so factual. I stay quiet, dumbfounded. While he lies relaxed on the meadow and looks at four young women who skip past us singing and dancing, I think to myself.

Ulrich made it sound so matter of fact as if my future did not depend on this question. Well, on the answer, actually. I should be satisfied with it. But I am not. Homosexuality will not exist in the monastery because I will not practice it. Is it really that simple? Will my irrepressible desire be conquered by the theoretic commandment of chastity alone? I still have my doubts.

Meanwhile, it seems that the time has passed to ask more questions, to dig deeper into my thoughts, and share more of myself. In any case, I wanted to clarify matters and, in so doing, gained a confidant in the monastery, so I achieved something.

Ulrich looks at his watch.

»Sorry, I have so little time. You can see how busy it is. I have to get back to the booth.«

Already? I thought we would have a little more time together.

»Yes, too bad. Thanks for taking the time.«

He shakes my hand.

»See you soon in Metten.«

During our handshake, I look at him carefully. Has my openness changed anything between us? I do not think so. He seems the same to me.

»It was nice to see you again and talk to you. I feel relieved now.«

He nodes and returns to his confreres.

Agitated but happy, I return to my friends. I do not share with them the subject of our conversation. Such is not the nature of our friendship that it has reached such depth. In a certain way, Ulrich, who already knows so much about me, is closer to me.

But they are great traveling companions, and I am looking forward to traveling to London and maybe even Scotland with them if the budget allows it and the rickety car holds up.

My wonderful vacation is hardly over, and I am already preparing to say farewell to my previous life. Saying goodbye to the people in my family who I am closest to is difficult for me. My Uncle Heiner, Aunt Anna, and cousin Marion have always been kind to me. Always ready with a kind word and a big piece of cake, even when at home, it felt like the sky had come falling down again.

Having announced my visit over the phone, a generously set coffee table awaits me upon my arrival. As soon as we take a seat, I know that not even my favorite cake will really taste good today.

»I've come to say goodbye...«

I cannot speak.

Aunt Anna's brown eyes fill with tears, even my usually hardy Uncle Heiner blinks suspiciously, and my cousin Marion looks at me with a startled face.

»Oh, boy, you sure have chosen a special path.«

Aunt Anna pats my hand and gives me a heaping serving of whipped cream.

»Aren't we going to see you anymore?« Marion asks, emotional.

»In the first year of the novitiate, there are no visits, no telephone calls, only letters.«

»Then you won't be around when Uncle Heiner celebrates his 50th birthday next year?«

Aunt Anna is visibly struggling to compose herself.

»I will think of you and write to him — I promise,« I vow with great seriousness, my fingers solemnly raised in an oath.

»What was his name again? The brother of your best friend's nephew? Was it Fredi? He also joined the monastery!« my uncle says, joining the conversation.

My aunt frowns.

»Fredi? The jack-of-all-trades? Never. You mean Conrad. The brother-in-law of Lieselotte's son.«

»That's right, Conrad. He went into the monastery too. It wasn't easy for him there, from what I heard.«

My uncle shakes his head thoughtfully. »It'll be quite an adjustment. But...« his face lightens up, »Armin knows what he's getting into. Come, Anna, give the boy another piece of cake. Who knows what he'll get to eat over there.«

As my aunt carefully nudges a particularly juicy slice of gooseberry pie onto my overloaded plate, she asks, »When are you leaving?«

»I have a little time left,« I say, chewing heartily. No one here objects if I speak with my mouth full.

»I'm heading out the day before my birthday. Right now, I'm packing my things. I want to take as little as possible with me.«

»You're doing all right. We always knew you were on the right track, right, Heiner?« says Aunt Anna, nodding wisely, with the cake server in her hand again. Gratefully, I decline her offer with a small wave.

»I always said that Armin would become a man of God. As often as he is in church,« remarks Uncle Heiner. Thankfully, he accepts the next piece of cake.

»Will you pray for us, please?« my cousin asks anxiously.

»Of course, I'll include you in my daily prayers.«

»And if you need anything, you'll let me know, promise?« Aunt Anna insists.

I am so touched I can only nod. That's why these two are my favorite relatives: they always hit the right note. And my aunt bakes the world's best gooseberry pie.

At home, I continue to prepare for my new life. I carefully sort out what I want to keep and put it in a suitcase; the rest I will give to Salvation Army. It is not difficult for me to clear out my closet, part with most of my books, and give away my bicycle.

On the other hand, the framed picture of our city church comes carefully packed in my suitcase. In honor of my Holy Communion, it has hung in the small prayer corner I had set up in my bedroom. The view of the baroque nave will remind me of my home parish while I am in Metten. On top of it, I put the rosary and the image of Christ. With that, my most important belongings are stowed away, and I feel strangely liberated: All ballast has been thrown off. I have reduced myself to the essential.

And then, I suddenly realize that I must go to the monastery the same way: with nothing but the clothes I wear on my body. Without a burden to weigh me down, without any luggage as I leave the house. Literally, not to be chauffeured or to travel by train in any reasonable comfort. Instead, I want to set off by foot on the path to my new life, approaching the monastery step by step, just as I am.

I am glad that Abbot Berthold understands when I tell him I will send my suitcase ahead.

»You want to do something clever, don't you, Armin? Give

your life to God in poverty, right? You have my blessing.«

My father's blessing too?

»What's this crazy idea?« they had said the night before when my father asked about my luggage.

»Where did that boy get that idea from?« my mother said, rubbing her hands nervously.

»Certainly not from my family. Walk to the monastery. Really ... and perhaps without a Pfenning in your pocket!«

»Of course,« I reply loud and clear, »otherwise, it doesn't make sense.«

»It doesn't make sense anyway, Armin. There's a train to Metten. A train. Nobody has to walk there nowadays. It's the 20th century.«

My father looked at me as if I had lost my mind. My mother shook her head in disbelief. This is not how I imagined this evening with my parents. I just want to go. And I'm infinitely happy when in the early morning hours, the time has finally come to leave. Emotional, the night before, I had said goodbye to my brothers and sisters. I do not have much more to say to my parents.

I look at my father in silence.

»Oh, Armin, I wish you the best.«

He clumsily embraces me and, at the same time, fiddles

with my jacket pocket. It crackles. What is he doing? As my father lets go of me, I cautiously feel the pocket from the outside through the thin fabric. There is something in there. Instead of looking, I hug my mother, who I will miss, even though I resent her for not taking my side last night.

She hugs me tight: »Take care, and God bless you, my boy.«

I tear myself away from her and leave my parents' house without turning back. On the way, I reach into my right jacket pocket and pull out a hundred Deutsche Mark bill. I look at the blue note, stunned. My father cannot take me seriously even one time!

I want to go to Metten without money. That is exactly what I said yesterday because I want to do that. It is so typical for him to try to foist it upon me anyway. As if I cannot take care of myself.

A thought comes to my mind: Of course, it is impossible to turn around and give him his money back. But that does not mean I have to keep it. I would rather spend it wisely. And I already know what I will do. One last time my way leads me to the early mass, presided over today by Father Ellinger. One last time I receive his blessing with the other parishioners. On my way out, I put Father's money in the offertory box, where it will be put to good use.

Relieved and cheerful, I can now begin my long journey.

My route will lead me through the Bavarian Forest, past the villages of Regen, Bayerisch Eisenstein, and Zwiesel to Metten. My plan is to arrive on August 14th, one day before Assumption Day.

On the way, I ask for food and shelter. I find whatever else I need as I go along. So alone with myself in nature, I feel completely free. Deeply I breathe in the musky smell of the dark woods. The splashing of countless little streams along the path sounds auspicious and rouses my vivid imagination. With each step, I seem to be more and more captivated by the unspoiled landscape; with each step, I find it harder to resist the sexual images that appear in a gnarled trunk or a stream. My thoughts are making me excited.

At the same time, as I know well enough, each step brings me closer to my future life as a monk. A life of abstinence. In the middle of all men.

Speaking of men. Back there, just after the bend in the road. The first hiker I met today. The determined step, the muscular arms, the full hair: he looked good – I like him. Our eyes crossed. I cannot help but look behind me. He does not look back.

Suddenly desperation takes hold of me. I slip into the deep thicket of the forest and ejaculate. Now I feel ashamed. Am I even worthy of the life I set out for? Or am I – literally – not on the right path?

Despite the warm temperatures, I am shivering, and my headaches. I would love to lie down right here on the moss, as tired and exhausted as I am. Instead, I pull myself together and move on. An important stretch of my journey lies ahead of me: I hope to cross the Kalteck Pass in the next few days.

After a night full of confused dreams, in the early morning, I know that my journey is already over. Every bone in my body seems to hurt, my forehead burns, and I hardly have the strength to descend the narrow staircase.

»My, boy, you don't look well at all,« I hear the corpulent landlady say, who was kind enough to give me shelter.

»Want some hot chocolate?«

»Perhaps a tea instead. And may I use your telephone?«

»I'll bring you a nice hot peppermint tea. It's just as well that you call your parents and have them come pick you up.«

I look at her with disgust. I'm sure her words are meant kindly, but they are completely unrealistic to me.

Call my parents? So that my father can get in the car and tell me himself what he always knew: »I told you right away: This isn't going to work!«

Never ever!

I only know one person who can help me now. I take a

small crumpled piece of paper from my pants pocket and dial the number of the monastery.

»Kloster Metten,« answers the deep voice of the old doorman.

»This is Armin Heining from Cham. May I please speak to Abbot Berthold?«

»Are you the Armin, who is on his way here by foot?« I can clearly hear the curiosity resonating in his voice.

»Yes, that's right. And that's why I must speak with the abbot.«

»One moment, I'll connect you.«

Rarely have I felt so discouraged and small as I did in that moment, waiting to confess to the abbot that I could not fulfill my ambitious plans. In my feverish delusion, I can hear my mother and her warning about this ›castle in the sky‹.

»Good morning, Armin. What's going on?« I hear Abbot Berthold say in his soothing voice.

»Good morning, Abbot Berthold. I have fallen ill and can no longer continue my journey on foot. Now I don't know what to do.«

»Where are you?«

I tell him the name and location of the inn.

»Good. Rest now. After lunch, I'll send Father Barnabas to

you by car. He'll pick you up.«

I sigh with relief.

»Thank you very much. And I'm sorry for the trouble I've caused you.«

»No problem, Armin; we want you to arrive safely.«

When I hung up the phone, I could hardly believe that I actually got away without a word of reproach. Nothing but kindness and goodness have been bestowed upon me in this dark hour. And a large cup of steaming peppermint tea.

A few hours later, Abbot Berthold sends Father Barnabas by car so that he can pay for my accommodation and drive me to the monastery. Metten is another twenty kilometers away.

The morning after my arrival at the monastery, which I had imagined to be completely different, I woke up at about eight o'clock in the guest room. Physically, I am back on my feet; a delicious soup and a lot of sleep have done their work. Emotionally, however, I am far from having recovered from my failure yesterday. For can it have been anything else? I allowed my lust to overwhelm me and weaken me so much that I could not make my way to the end. How embarrassing to have to ask for help simply because I could not control myself. No wonder my parents do not believe in me. I wonder what the others might be thinking. In my fragile state, I had been taken straight to the guest room.

»Get some sleep first, Armin. A good sleep is still the best medicine,« Abbot Berthold told me consolingly during my warm welcome. Father Barnabas had then led me through the empty corridors to the second floor and brought me a small meal. I had not yet seen other monks. Not even Ulrich. I wonder what he will say.

The last time we met was at the wonderful Catholic day, where I had asked him how homosexuality fits into monastic life.

And now this. I can't control myself. Well, I'm not celibate yet; I'm not a monk. Nevertheless, I expected from myself that perhaps the conversation with Ulrich would bring about some kind of change for the better. As a kind of preparation for being a monk, so to speak.

Instead, nothing happened. In this regard, nothing has changed. It's all the same as before. My desire cannot be reconciled with my ideals. In fact, they seem to contradict each other. This is precisely why I could not continue my journey alone but had to ask for help in a guilty and abject way. For this, I am ashamed.

Will Ulrich again be able to tell how agitated I am? During my first visit, it sometimes seemed as if he could see inside me; the way his answers felt so heartfelt.

I sigh deeply, say a quick prayer to God, and simply hope

for a quiet first day in Metten. I wish only for a smooth start and to find my place in the community.

I hope the monastic silence will settle over my restless spirit and help me to find inner peace.

But first, my growling stomach reminds me of what I want most urgently: breakfast. I quickly wash myself, get dressed, and walk to the dining room.

The closer I get to the refectory, the more nervous I get. Before I open the door, I take a deep breath. Who will I meet? But only Father Wilhelm is there, wiping crumbs off the table.

»Ah, yes, hello to you. Nice to have you with us.«

He comes up to me, clutches my hand with both hands, and shakes warmly.

»I'm happy to be here too, at last,« I reply happily.

The prudent Father Barnabas takes me aside after breakfast: »I'll show you your cell now. Your suitcase awaits you there.«

With an amused look at my dusty clothes, he adds: »Before we go to the tailor shop, I'm sure you'll want fresh trousers and a clean shirt.«

I look down at myself and can only agree with him.

At the end of the long corridor on the familiar second floor is my own first monastery cell, an inviting room on the west side, about ten meters square and freshly painted. The smell of paint still hangs in the air.

»Bright, wide, comfortable« are my first thoughts. The large window opens directly onto the rambling monastery gardens. To the left at the back, almost under the window, there is a narrow bed; next to it on the wall, a solid wardrobe, and a wash basin and mirror right next to the door. On the right is a still-empty bookshelf, a simple desk is set crosswise, and a small brown carpet lies in the middle of the room. At first sight, I feel at home.

»Very nice! I like it here,« I call out and look at Barnabas enthusiastically.

»Good. Get yourself settled in, and in one hour, we'll go to the tailor's.«

The way to my first tunic fitting feels rather hazardous and risky as I try not to lose my balance on the worn-out steps of the narrow staircase. In the ›monastic creaking‹ of the wooden steps, the rotten wood does not go unnoticed. The handrail seems so fragile that I hardly dare to hold on. Back when I visited the monastery, Ulrich had only pointed to the compact building in passing and referred to the »monastic power station with a water turbine and tailoring.« Now I am experiencing firsthand what he was talking about.

High up under the crooked roof, accessible only via steep

stairs is the realm of the monastery tailor Herr Seidl, a lively man from the village.

»Mr. Seidl belongs to the monastery like an inventory,« Barnabas whispered to me before I dared to climb up under the roof.

»Greetings, Mr. Seidl. We have a new candidate. And he needs something from you,« Barnabas says, pushing me towards the old man.

»Yes, hello to you. Where'd you come from? What's your name?«

He deftly pulls out the measuring tape and measures my height, the width of my shoulders, neck, and belly, and the length of my arms.

While I talk a little bit about myself, I look in amazement at the abundance of black fabric that seems to flood the small room. On long coat hangers hang densely packed black robes, which all look the same at first glance. There are, in fact, two kinds: with and without folds, neatly sorted.

As soon as Mr. Seidl has taken all my measurements, he chooses an undergarment from the collection of habits with a sure grip: »Well, let's see what we have for you. «

With a critical look, he holds it in front of my body and mumbles in strong Lower Bavarian dialect: »Well, that might just fit.«

Of course, he is right: The first tunic clings to my body like a glove. It feels special because it represents a separation from my former life, insecurity, self-doubt, and fear of failure.

»You look smart. Suits you,« Father Barnabas says happily.

I am sincerely grateful for these appreciative words.

In fact, my whole first day was marked by a deep sense of gratitude, as it turns out that my concerns from the morning proved to be completely unfounded. None of the brothers look at me sideways or make fun of the inglorious end of my lofty plans.

They all welcome me into their circle. This wonderful feeling will surely carry me for a long time to come.

»Hello. Welcome. I'm glad you're here! You've made it to the monastery after all!«

Ulrich. I did not see him coming. He was surely at mass this morning, but there had been no opportunity for conversation afterwards. Now he is standing next to me. He was not here when I arrived because his holidays overlapped with my first days in the monastery.

»Hello.«

The insecurity of the first day, which I thought I had left behind, suddenly comes back – as if Ulrich had actually been given the ability to look into my soul. At first, I did not know how to deal with it.

He already knows a lot about me. And somehow, I still fear he might deduce something that could compromise me.

The news that Father Barnabas had to bring me to the monastery probably got around to him already. I hope that we can leave this rather delicate matter for the time being.

Perhaps Brother Ulrich has some inkling of how I feel because this first conversation that he has with me as a future novice actually takes a pleasantly shallow turn: He tells a little about his holiday, and I recall the sense of belonging to the monastic community that overwhelmed me on my very first visit.

»But to live with you from now on here at Metten makes me very happy.«

»We are happy to have you with us. And if you ever have a question whose answer you can't find in the Rule of St. Benedict, please feel free to ask me. Perhaps I can help.«

His smile is heartfelt, and I know my fears were unfounded. Brother Ulrich sees in me only a deeply spiritual future brother. Nothing else matters.

Because I entered the monastery in 1980, the year of the Jubilee of the founder of the order, there was a sense of celebration all around. On the occasion of the one thousand five hundredth birthday of St. Benedict of Nursia, Abbot Berthold had traveled to the Abbey of Montecassino, the original monastery of the Benedictine Order, south of Rome. There he had met with Pope John Paul II.

During the investiture, he delivers a message from the Pope that he and everyone in the church and in the world expect the Benedictines to be true monks in the spirit of their religious father. They truly seek God, love, and rejoice him, separated from the world but living united with their brothers in the world through the communion of love. Moreover, they live in the trusted framework of obedience and love, arising from peace and joy. So that in the house of God, no one may be confused and sad.

These words of the Pope speak directly to my heart. Have I not sought God and experienced his immediate closeness here in Metten? A place where my love for him may finally find expression. To leave my parent's house and follow God's call to live in the monastery in all humbleness and modesty seems now like an obvious decision. Only here have I found the community that I had always dreamed of: where I am welcome, even if I am disheveled and blown in by the wind. Whose brothers, in my imperfection, accept me as one of theirs – as the one, I want to be: a monastic brother like them. Our love for God unites us. In the cloister and in the outside world.

In order to leave behind once and for all the turmoil of lust and the struggle of my life, I will lead a spiritual life according to the Rule of the Order. I will find inner peace only by strictly following this path in the footsteps of Saint Benedict. In him, I recognize my purpose.

Of course, part of this new life is to discard my worldly identity and choose a new name, my religious name. The abbot gives us postulants a say in the naming process. I have set myself the aim of desiring to recognize Christ and serve him. I also think back to my arduous walk from Cham to Metten and the patron saint who must have been watching over me. With this in mind, I submit my proposal to Abbot Berthold.

Today the monastic community will learn the religious name I have chosen: ›Christoph‹. Together with another brother, I am clothed by Abbot Berthold in the black habit of the order. He first puts the collar around my neck. He puts the tunic on over my civilian clothes; it is pulled over my head and strapped with the cingulum. This is followed by the scapular, a black cloth symbolizing the yoke of Christ. He pulls it over my head and straightens it on my shoulders. It reaches almost to the ground in front and behind.

The sacred meaning is clear to me. Take my yoke upon you, and learn from me, for I am gentle and lowly in heart, and you will find rest for your souls. For my yoke is easy, and my burden is light. (Gospel of Matthew, chapter 17, verses 28-30). When the abbot finally fastened the hood to my collar, I felt uplifted, a completely as a new person.

Abbot Berthold's words at the end of the ceremony are particularly moving when he emphasized that life as a disciple of St. Benedict is an excellent opportunity to follow Christ. He was enthused by how concrete and closely the love of God and the next is connected and what a variety of paths open up in this school to serve peace!

Soon my monastic life will range between daily prayer and active charity, faithful to our motto ›Ora et labora‹ (Pray and Work). Each novice is assigned a task according to their aptitude and inclination.

»For you and Rhabanus, I have entrusted you the care of our brother Nathan. You know that he was once our doctor and is now suffering from severe dementia. You must look after him, take care of his hygiene and bring him food or take him to the refectory if he is physically able.«

Because I once did an internship at the hospital in Cham during the school holidays, Abbot Berthold considers me appropriate for the care of the elderly brother. Together with Rhabanus, the other novice, I look after the worthy monk in the last years of his life.

What I experienced for the first time years ago during my visit here now determines my daily life: Not only the prayer ceremonies, the meaning, and sequence of which I now study, but also the good company of the young brothers. The monastic routine corresponds so much to my inner longing for stability and clear structure that, miraculously, even getting up early in the morning is not difficult for me. With each day that I spend with my brothers in the congregation, the impression of having found my inner home is intensified.

You've finally reached your destination, right?

This line reaches me one day in a letter from Aunt Anna. Although I don't write as diligently because I am too involved in my new daily structure, she often thinks of me and keeps me regularly informed about the latest developments in her letters. Or she shares her idea about what my life in the monastery is like. We are so happy for you that your long journey was worthwhile. And that you have achieved what you so much desired.

Already arrived at my destination? Not by a long shot. I know that I am just at the beginning. University studies alone will take several years – and I have not even started yet. Above all, I have to prove my eligibility as a monk. In the coming years, whether I lead a disciplined life will be repeatedly examined.

I feel confident about the future because an important sense of achievement is already emerging: sexuality is no longer an issue for me – thanks to the habit's sheer lack of attraction. It makes us all look equal, without contours. There is only black, flowing material, no trigger to stimulate my senses. Lust finally no longer throws me off my course, allowing me to concentrate on my daily duties. The strict rhythm of praying and working do the rest to keep my libido in check. As Novice Frater Christoph, I lead an exemplary life in harmony with myself.

Armin (Brother Christoph OSB) in his Monks Robe

Chapter 3: A Shadow Calls

One year later, things are still going well. I am not tempted by sexual thoughts anymore. I have found my place in the community. My whole life seems to have come together. This inner change is also visible on the outside: the insecure high school graduate and self-doubting nerd no longer exists. I have not returned to my former life, to my family, or to my old habits. On October 30, 1981, I vowed nothing less than to maintain this status as I committed myself to the Metten Monastery for another three years.

I have invited my parents, siblings, and favorite relatives to attend this ceremony. I want them all to witness how I vow, albeit for three years, to live my life strictly according to the Rule of Saint Benedict.

»Oh boy!«

As usual, my beaming Aunt Anna has the right words for the moment.

»Now you are an adult and so confident!«

Even Uncle Heiner's opinion is quite heartfelt.

I have not seen them for more than a year, of course. That makes changes all the more noticeable except as regards my parents. They seem the same. Still, I think I hear a bit of pride.

»You're going to be something after all, boy. I didn't think so.«

My father places his hand on my shoulder. I suppose it is a sign of his appreciation.

Embarrassed, I turn to my mother, who nods and looks moved.

Indeed, I feel confident as I look towards an orderly future: I will begin my theological studies in just a few days. When I graduated in 1986, I will be ordained a priest for the monastery. I am ready.

To everyone's surprise, Abbot Berthold has decided to revive an almost forgotten Metten tradition this year.

»You two will not attend university in Salzburg. You'll go to Würzburg, to my alma mater.«

A side glance at Ulrich was enough to tell me he was as taken aback as I was. He completed his first theology degree in Austria and expected to pursue his teaching degree there as well.

»You will attend the St. Benedict College of the Münsterschwarzach Monks in Würzburg. During the semester, you will live there together with students from other monastic communities.«

Privately, I had assumed that Ulrich and I would have rooms next to each other – and somewhat disappointed that I would not live outside the cloister like him. But he has already taken his solemn vows and is a priest, whereas I am still at the very beginning of my monastic career, so apparently, I need more monastic oversight. My room on the fourth floor under the roof is even smaller than my monastery cell and, unfortunately a bit cramped due to the steep pitch of the roof. There is not even enough space for a wash basin. On the other hand, I look directly at the treetops and can see residential neighborhoods in the distance. Altogether the accommodation is comfortable, and I am satisfied.

In terms of style, the plain concrete building of the college has nothing in common with the dignified baroque splendor of the Metten monastery. The two wings of the building are set at a right angle to each other, directly on two streets, one of which is very busy. Even though the inner courtyard with its tall trees is closed off by a wall and looks like a green oasis, the amount of ambient noise makes it difficult to compare to the countryside around a small Bavarian town – and certainly to the seclusion of my home monastery. Compared to the approximate three thousand people who live in Metten, I have now arrived in a big city.

And here, things are different: ›Ora et labora‹ is suddenly no longer as strict as at home but is instead adapted to the framework of the city and the demands of studying: We do not get up at four-forty but at six. The daily prayer times are reduced from five to three, all are recited in German, and only one is sung. Instead of table readings, there is open conversation during meals.

Ulrich and I have agreed to go for a walk every Sunday afternoon. For the time being, he is still my closest friend in the new community, not only because we are members of the same monastery. Again and again, I have trusted his advice; I hope he will have some useful tips for me as a first-year student.

Our lectures and seminars take place at the nearby Julius-Maximilian University. If we manage, I walk the short distance to the first lecture in the morning with Ulrich.

»Look over there. What are they doing?«

Curious, I stop on the grass to watch the small group of men and women practicing carefully flowing exercises. It looks like they are moving their arms and legs in slow motion.

»Tai Chi,« Ulrich replies succinctly.

»Interesting,« I say, glad to have learned something new.

»It's not interesting. It goes back to early Chinese martial arts.« The strictness of his tone discourages me from pursuing it further.

In silence, we continue to the Department of Catholic Theology. Behind the historical facade is a modern atrium, from which corridors branch off that confuse me at first. A very foreign world, one in which I often lose my orientation. The representation of this seems to be the countless papers, large and small, colorful and white, which are glued, pinned, or stapled one next to the other or on top of each other as if the whole room were a bulletin board. A hopeless hodgepodge of requests, event announcements, calls, and invitations.

If only somebody would clean up this mess, I think. You don't know where to look first, I say to myself angrily as I pass by. The more I look at it, the more I recognize what this hullabaloo really means to me: a mirror of myself, for I have been struggling with nothing more than unprecedented chaos, chaos of emotions, for quite some time now. Unfortunately, student life in Würzburg does not agree with me at all.

The blessing of having more free time to complete my homework is now proving to be a curse. I could never write enough reports and seminar papers that I could reproduce the rigorous structure of my everyday life back in Metten, which makes me the exemplary novice I want to be. It feels like; without consistent withdrawal from the world, I am somehow denied access to my true being. How can I succeed in my studies in Würzburg? There is always something going on here. I constantly see new faces and have to adjust to new challenges.

And then there are these young men, uncovered by robes,

which I encounter all the time at the university. I am overstimulated and do not know how to deal with it. Naturally, I try to collect myself in private prayer as often as possible, but my suffering is not getting any better. Mentally I am in pain because I can no longer center myself.

I do not want to ask Ulrich for advice. Sometimes I feel like I have lost touch with him. Perhaps he is just too busy with his studies. Unfortunately, he hasn't yet found the time for our planned walks on Sunday. Instead, I see him quite often with the rather handsome Gregor.

I decided to ask the spiritual counselor for help. Here in the college, the role of the spiritual counselor is held by Father Claudius, who is also the rector of the house. He seems sensitive and sympathetic. Surely, he will know what to do.

I arrive at his office on the first floor punctually at the agreed time. Because time is short, I get straight to the point.

»I'm having trouble settling in. Everything is so different here compared to Metten. It's a mystery to me how to get a foothold here without my usual organized routine as I know it from the monastery.«

It's impossible to be clearer. But I feel a rift inside me. I cannot possibly tell the honorable monk everything.

»That is not at all unusual. It was the same when I first came to study. Most freshmen probably feel the same way.«

Father Claudius radiates an incredible calmness and smiles at me. I don't think that we are talking about the same thing.

»During your studies, you will discover completely new worlds of experience. They can be quite overwhelming. There is more freedom here, and you have to learn to deal with it because less is predetermined. Find out what you're interested in and which inclination you'd like to pursue. What do you need in order to realize your potential?«

I do not know what to say. I was not expecting this kind of response.

»Study should always mean self-study: discovering yourself and realizing your potential. Each course of study becomes its own path to self-awareness.«

Study as self-awareness? I have never heard Abbot Berthold say such a thing.

»Discover and explore your inner spaces, then design them yourself! Make something of them, make something of yourself, of your possibilities!«

I was really hoping for some practical advice, something like ›withdraw more often in prayer by yourself.‹ Then I would have known what to do.

»And one more thing: It is always a matter of critically examining oneself, of constantly reflecting: What have I contributed to my situation being the way it is? Looking down into the depths of the soul is of decisive importance, as is the exchange of the knowledge gained. Only then can the supposedly absurd be clarified.«

This is certainly not a teaching that anyone in my monastery would approve of. My head is spinning, and I feel like I have been somehow left alone in my distress.

»Be patient with yourself. Just see what you are interested in and let yourself be stimulated. I'll give you special...«

There's a knock at the door. Another Brother has a question – my time is up.

Unfortunately, the busy Father Claudius does not continue the sentence he began but says a heartfelt farewell to me instead.

More helpless than at the beginning of the conversation, I try to make sense of it back in my room. It was absolutely unprecedented; never had I heard a monk speak like that before. It is unimaginable that such a conversation could have taken place in Metten. I pause for a moment, and my breath stops.

Yes: Such a conversation could never have taken place in Metten. At Metten, I don't gaze into an abyss. In the closely interwoven routines, I am reassured every day that I am on the right path. I want nothing more. Würzburg's laissez-faire attitude, on the other hand, threatens to turn me into a failure.

Once again, I feel like the aimless, insecure student who has not yet found his place.

But is that not exactly why I came to Würzburg – to learn? Here I am to visit the ›school of life‹. That is what Aunt Anna had called the experiences she would have gladly done without.

The question is, of course: What do I do now? If only I had more clues. Unfortunately, I did not find out what Father Claudius wanted to give me before I left. The only practical advice that I might have been able to put to use failed to reach me.

Still brooding, I sit at the table during dinner. I can hardly wait for the waiters to clear the table, and we have the after-dinner prayer. I want to go back to my room.

Father Claudius taps hard on the table. We get up and pray together. Unexpectedly, Father Claudius knocks again on the table and says to everyone, »I have another announcement to make. Tonight, after the Night Prayer, there will be another open Eutony evening. Those who wish to attend, please meet in the Blue Room at eight fifteen«.

Illuminated by a sudden flash of lightning, I see a path forward: This is it. That's where I have to go! Thrilled by this blazing realization, I turn to Ulrich.

»I'll stop by there later on. Do you want to come?«

He raises his eyebrows, »Are you serious? Why?«

»Because I'm curious to know what it is. And Father Claudius is leading the evening.«

Ulrich looks at me as if he misheard.

»This newfangled stuff doesn't do any good.«

He turns to Gregor, thunderstruck. »Isn't that right?« he says.

Gregor frowns and nods his head.

I stick to my opinion: »I would like to try it. I'm here to learn, to get to know new things.«

»But this does not include reform education, of course. You're here for your studies in theology. That's the way it's supposed to be.« Ulrich looks at me as if he sees me for the first time.

»I know,« I reply quietly, but I am unable to yield. »But why can't I…«

Ulrich interrupts me: »Christoph, this is not a discussion. You know how I feel.«

He leans over to Gregor, whispering.

I should have just kept my mouth shut. Ulrich had already spoken badly about ›monks who don't know where their places are‹ once before. At the time, I did not really understand what he meant. Now I assume that he was referring to the monks from Münsterschwarzach, who are obviously taking a different path from ours at Metten.

At the same time, I am aware that I must not take Ulrich's harsh words to heart. If he knew about my emotional distress, if he could get the whole picture, he would certainly have reacted more sensitively – as he always did. I am quite sure of that.

I was apparently the only new one, the only person who joined the group without any previous experience.

»That doesn't matter at all. Everyone decides for themselves when it's the right time for them to turn to their own bodies with goodwill. We are happy, Brother Christoph, that you have found your way to us today.«

Alone these friendly words of greeting from Father Claudius were themselves the purest healing for my soul.

»In this workshop, we will dedicate ourselves to a learning process in which you will gain a completely new awareness of your body regarding the possibilities of its expression and movements and its physiological processes. You will experience the influence of the external world on your body tension. Or in an adaptation of a word by Gerda Alexander, the founder of this new pedagogy: What does a touch do to me? To what extent does what I touch, touch me?«

I catch my breath. Is touch the solution to the mystery of my life?

Soon I find myself in unfamiliar exercises in which, by touching the ground, I learn to empathize with my skin as a large, living sense organ. I am told that ›in the sensual contact of my skin with the outer world‹, I become aware of how the environment affects me. I hear something about an influence on my ›inner vibration‹ and on the tension of my muscles, which are connected to my skin by countless nerve tracks.

Pretty soon, I reach the limit of my comprehension, can no longer follow, and lose my way. I have never had to take the course in this direction before: It is strange to observe what the touch of a mattress does to me. Today I heard about 'body space consciousness' for the first time.

I can hardly believe that I am actually lying here, focusing on 'the psychosomatic dimension' of my being. The phrase alone that such a thing even exists is unbelievable! At least I don't feel any worse than when I started.

When it is over, Albin, Clemens, and Humbert come up to me. Up to now, we have not had much contact. Now I am glad that they have come to talk to me.

»Well, Christoph. How did you like it?« inquires Brother Humbert, a lively, blond monk from the Münsterschwarzach Abbey.

»Yes, quite well, thank you. I had no idea what to expect,« I reply, a little nervous.

»You probably have some questions about the new realm you've just discovered,« says the ever-cheerful Brother Clemens as he smiles at me warmly. He also is a member of the same Abby as Brother Humbert.

»Shall we sit down?« Brother Albin says, taking the lead and directing us to the sofa in the corner. He is a senior in theology and an overachiever, so unlike me.

As soon as we sit down, Brother Humbert brings mugs and a pot of hot tea.

»What does ›Eutony‹ mean, anyway?« I blurt out immediately. »Where does the word come from?« I turn intuitively to Albin.

»The first syllable is derived from the Greek word ›eu,‹ which can be translated as ›well‹ or ›harmonious.‹ The second syllable refers to the word ›tonus‹ for ›tension.‹ Eutony is about creating a ›tension of well-being‹ within the body, one which is completely oriented towards one's own being. He who in resting can feel so secure about himself that he can flourish in the world in a completely different way – in his behavior with his fellow human beings, or in his dealings with himself.«

Does that not sound perfect and desirable? But would Ulrich approve? I cannot get what he said out of my head.

»I invited brother Ulrich from my monastery to come along, but he said Eutony is reform education. Is there any truth to that?«

Albin nods cautiously. »I know the discussion,« he says, and the tone of his voice tells me what he thinks.

»I don't use that term at all; I prefer to say that eutony and new forms of education all follow the same idea: to understand each person as a unique personality, for whom there is no prefabricated form in which to fit in. There is only one way to explore your being and find out where you want to go: your own way.«

»In theory, it sounds good,« I reply cautiously. »It's just that I've had some other experiences.« It's important to me to be as open and truthful as possible. »So I question whether I might become a black sheep again in the midst of a herd of well-behaved white sheep if I show myself as I truly am. Do I really fit in here? In the end, I didn't have much to say. You were all so articulate in the final round.«

Clemens answers kindly. »You are mistaken, Christoph. We've just been practicing a little longer than you. Humbert, you have the most experience out of the three of us, don't you?«

Humbert nods amusedly. »That was your first encounter with Eutony today,« he says. »It usually takes some time to get used to, and at first, you don't know what to say.«

»I can only agree,« Albin confirms with his usual

seriousness. »Especially if you come from a traditional monastery. Then bodywork is something completely new and unusual. Don't put yourself under pressure. Eutony is a long, lively process. If you think it could be something for you, just drop by again next time.«

I can only agree with Albin. »Exactly. The two weeks will give me time to process my impressions.« And until then, I first have to think it over. I feel the urgent need to catch my breath.

»Sometimes, the three of us meet up earlier.« Clemens says, smiling. »If the two weeks are too long for us until the next official date.«

»Gee, Clemens, that's a good idea: Christoph can come next week, too, when we meet at your place.«

Humbert looks eagerly first at Clemens and then at me.

»Don't push it, Humbert,« says Albin, dampening his euphoria. »Let Christoph do it his way. He'll come and see us when he feels up to it.«

»That's what I meant.« Humbert makes a gesture with his hand, underlining his surprise.

»Perhaps, but it wasn't so clear,« replies Albin, like a schoolmaster.

Humbert looks at me as if to say: ›He's always like that.‹

I put my cup down. I had hardly touched my tea because I had been excited and talking so much.

»Thanks for the invitation. I'll let you know.«

I say goodbye hastily, almost too fast. I need to be alone for a while, in peace.

»Oh, Christoph!« I hear Clemens shout before I make it to the door.

»Yes?«

I turn around.

»All sheep are welcome in our flock. The white, the black, and the colorful. Don't forget.«

He winks at me.

I cannot help smiling. »I'll remember that.«

Back in my room, I immediately reach for my diary to try to get a better picture: What did I learn today? What will I take with me from this evening? And what can Eutony do for me?

»We respect who you are in this moment, completely independent of your inner place. We welcome each person in their own way.«

First, I have to write down this great sentence from Albin. As if he and the others would understand exactly where I am inwardly now – and everything would be all right. Even though they have no idea of the mess, I look at when I look inside myself. But Albin put my dilemma in a nutshell: Metten is conservative, of course. So what would my brothers think of me if I described how I was stretched out on the floor, working on the sensitization of my body perception? What might Abbot Berthold think of the path to a ›eutony of the whole personality?‹

Taking part is, of course, a daring endeavor. How many people might I offend if I keep going in this direction? I can understand Ulrich's resentment. My father once called progressive education ›anti-authoritarian nonsense‹.

But my father is far away, and Ulrich spends his time with Gregor. I simply must use the freedom to work on myself and to understand more, to advance my self-study, as Father Claudius advised me to do. Albin would probably call it the study of myself. It is also hard to find something wrong with a method that teaches me to live in harmony with myself, to dissolve the contradiction between body and mind. I should be grateful for such a lesson, which might mean the end of my profound crisis. And not in another two weeks. Full of eagerness and newfound drive, I accepted the invitation from Albin, Clemens, and Humbert the next day.

With them, I dive into a whole new world full of unexpected possibilities and great opportunities. I think the best time of my life in Würzburg starts right now. I haven't felt this radiant in a long time. Is it the eutonic experience on my skin? I have not been participating for all that long.

Nevertheless, I can already feel myself approaching an inner balance. My body follows my mind. And it urges it to unfold in a completely new way and to discover another form of body consciousness that is not filled with guilt, shame, or timidity, and that gives me inner peace.

»You want to spread your wings...« Humbert said happily when I got back to them.

Yes, I suppose that is what it is. In any case, it feels like a wonderful coincidence to have come into contact with Humbert, Clemens, and Albert. Under their wings, I first realized what a hermit-like existence I led in my first weeks in Würzburg.

Moreover, I finally understand that I need to take more initiative than simply praying or hoping that someone will take me for a walk if I want to find out who I really am.

»Christoph, I've been looking for you!«

Ulrich appears suddenly as I am quickly turning the corner into the side wing. Lately, time is always so short.

»The spring weather is so beautiful. Would you like to go for a walk? We've been planning this for a while. Now is a good time for me.«

»Today? Of all days,« I want to say.

»Ah, I see.« I'm looking for the right words, embarrassed.

»It's really nice of you to ask.«

Ulrich nods benignly.

»But, unfortunately, I have a previous engagement.«

Without apparent disappointment, he replies, »Yes, then there is nothing to be done. I was just asking.«

Well, that settles that. I want to move on quickly, but he does not budge.

»What are you doing today?«

Plainly, I tell him: »I'm on my way to see Albin to talk about Ludwig.«

»You're gossiping with Albin about the librarian? Why?«

I have to laugh, which seems to annoy Ulrich even more.

»Not Brother Ludwig. I was talking about Ludwig Wittgenstein.«

»You're reading Wittgenstein, the linguistic philosopher?«

Ulrich stares at me in disbelief.

»One hears of such things, but I really wouldn't have thought it possible. You have come a long way, Christoph.«

Without suspicion, I'm delighted by his compliment: »Haven't I? Albin says the same thing.«

»Oh, is Brother Albin in charge of your studies now?« Ulrich seems stunned.

»So to speak. Albin recommended that I attend the lecture 'Religion and Existence'. And then I just followed my curiosity like Alice down the rabbit hole and came across Wittgenstein.«

Ulrich literally flinches when I talk about Alice in Wonderland.

»Are you serious, Christoph?«

»Of course.« That is exactly how I have finally made some progress.

»I can only wonder what you're wasting your time on.«

»What for? The name means something to you, too. Have you not read the ›Philosophical Investigations?‹

I noticed that I was being insubordinate.

»I studied the Holy Scriptures in my second semester. I see from your reaction that you are far too young and lack the background knowledge to properly classify works far outside your field of study.«

That's splitting hairs. One should not wait indefinitely when they already have the opportunity to educate themselves, Father Claudius told me.

»But I find it interesting...«

Ulrich interrupts me abruptly: »You and your interests! It would be nice if you would study your own assignments with the same zeal, Brother Christoph!«

»...and Father Claudius also approves of us expanding our horizons. We could never begin to open our minds early

enough; he said the other day at the end of the Eutonic Circle.«
I just kept talking as if he had not objected.

The unsightly furrows on Ulrich's forehead deepen.

»Oh, you're actually going there, too.«

»Of course, regularly.«

Just talking about it makes me happy: »Won't you come and try it? You'd never imagine how good you can feel in your own body.«

»I thought I already told you my opinion on such activities.«

I think I really riled him up now. I can see a small throbbing vein at his temple.

»Oh, that's right, I forgot. Well, I've got to get going. I hate to keep Albin waiting; he's always so busy.«

As I walk on, I call out to the visibly stunned Ulrich. »Let's just have a look on one of the next Sundays or so. Maybe something will come up then.«

And already, I am making my way down the next corridor.

My days are now so tightly organized that I often don't know where my head is anymore. I do not even seem to find the time in the evening to write down the day's thoughts. In particular, it is Humbert who invites me again and again to the sermons of the Münsterschwarzachers or recommends one of their small book publications because he notices how this entirely new world of faith fascinates me. The abbey in Münsterschwarzach is completely different from our own in Metten. This community is much more progressive than ours in Metten.

»Christoph!«

I look back, baffled.

Albin is standing outside his room, calling after me.

»You walked right past my door. And you're twelve minutes late!«

When Albin blames you, you feel very tiny, Clemens had said the other day when he was the target of Albin's reproach.

»Sorry! I was lost in thought.«

I shouldn't have let Ulrich keep me so long. Guiltily and with my head lowered, I enter Albin's room, which is crammed with books. To clear my favorite seat, I must move a stack of Latin anthologies onto the windowsill. Only now do I notice how exhausted I am. In fact, all I want is to be alone with myself. But first, there is Wittgenstein, of course.

I will hardly find the opportunity for introspection in the near future either because another youth vesper will be held in the Münsterschwarzach monastery. And I am very much looking forward to it – the privilege to hear Father Friedrich preach is a very special gift: I never heard such an interpretation of the Holy Scripture before. Even the biblical interpretation of the Münsterschwarzach monastery follows fundamentally different rules. In Father Friedrich's interpretation, there is something contemporary in the texts, and they reflect experiences that are familiar to me. It is impressive how he succeeds again and again in bringing us closer to the psychological depth of the Holy Scriptures.

If only this internal energy and contentment would last! The sense of being torn apart has once again returned to me. Despite my efforts, despite trying so much, I still have not achieved a lasting inner balance. Am I really on the right path? If only I knew what could give me lasting peace of mind. The Münsterschwarzacher holistic approach even includes Initiation Therapy. Maybe this could be a way for me to better understand my own true self and will help me become happy with myself. There is even supposed to be a lively dialogue with Count Karlfried Graf Dürckheim, one of the founders of this method.

I have heard from Clemens that Count Dürckheim not only dealt intensively with Zen practice during his long stay in Japan, but he also worked out its analogy to Christian mysticism. Such connections are not exactly obvious. What a privilege to be able to discuss these ideas with the teacher himself. Compared to reading abstract secondary sources, such an experience is of a completely different quality when it comes to gaining a deeper understanding. If I want to get even closer to real knowledge, maybe such a path is right for me.

»Oh, excuse me!«

On the stairs, I almost ran into this gaunt middle-aged monk because I – once again in a hurry – hardly looked where I was going. The brother gives me a frosty look, nods his head, and continues on his way.

At the bottom of the stairs, Humbert waits for me as planned. He looks especially cheerful today. »Do you know who you just walked into, Christoph?«

I try to think, but it's no use. I would not have forgotten that ascetic man.

»No, not that I remember.«

»That's Father Anton!« Humbert blurts out.

Oh, Father Anton. A Benedictine monk and Zen master, he lived in Japan for six years, studying Buddhism. Enlightened by Zen meditation, he then reinterpreted the writings of Christian mysticism.

»As of today, he is here in the college because he will oversee the construction of the House of St. Benedict,« Humbert reports.

As far as I know, the former boarding school is now being converted into Father Anton's place of work, the future House of St. Benedict: a course and conference center with a large Japanese-style meditation room, a small chapel, further practice rooms, a dining room, and overnight accommodations.

»As soon as he got here, he started asking everyone if they wanted to participate in his meditations.«

Humbert sounds positively gleeful.

»Yes, so? I thought we might like to try it, too.«

Humbert opens his eyes in surprise. »Really, Christoph… Weren't you listening to Albin?« Humbert asks, thunderstruck.

This may well be true since Albin not only likes to talk a lot, but he also likes to hear himself talk.

When I don't answer, Humbert fills in: »Buddhist Zen meditation is closer to heresy than to the Catholic Church.«

Yes, I remember now. It was something like that. A strong warning from Albin against »false prophets and their blasphemous methods.« In fact, I had been looking forward to hearing about the wisdom Father Anton brought back to us from the Far East.

But if Albin has his doubts – even though I seem to have suppressed them – it might be better to refrain for the time being. Albin's convictions are always sound.

»Yes, you're right,« I say as regretfully as I can.

»We should stay away from it,« says Humbert, nodding contentedly.

When would I have found the time to go there? I ask myself, self-critically. Recently I started to take an active part in the Eucharist celebrations here, which means regular meetings during the week to rehearse the prayer choreography. For the monks in Münsterschwarzach, seeking new forms of prayer is a self-evident interpretation of the Benedictine Rule. In seeking, for example, an encounter with God through simple, continuously repeating dance movements, in which I try to follow along and find my way, inch by inch.

Moreover, since I started bringing my eutonic knowledge into everyday life, I have started to experience the daily choir prayers as a spiritual experience that permeates the whole body and makes me feel especially close to God.

I have even taken Ulrich's reservations seriously, even if I doubt that he has any interest in my activities. Would he be pleased if he knew that I was not neglecting my theological studies? As part of the seminar ›On the Theory and Practice of Prayer,‹ I recently presented an exemplary seminar paper with the beautiful title ›Dance and the Encounter with God — a Relational-Theological Reflection on the Phenomenon of Dance‹. It was awarded the highest grade. Isn't it wonderful how I can combine my private interests with my studies? I am proud of myself.

Less enjoyable is experiencing the increasing division within the college.

»Either you are for Father Anton or against Father Anton,« Albin recently said in his apodictic tone that nips any contradiction in the bud.

»Borders of faith do not mark a middle course. Those who want to overcome them question the Catholic faith and challenge Rome. I think we'd all agree on that.«

Clemens and Humbert nod eagerly while I prefer not to take a stand at all. I observe from a distance the atmosphere of upheaval that began to prevail over the college recently, ever since Father Anton began promoting turning away from discursive thinking as I know it from prayer. According to him, a true mystical experience of enlightenment and inner unity is only possible in the wordless and objectless Zen meditation, turned away from the experience of the ego. Privately, I am impressed by the impersonal-looking monk's ability to gather fellow believers around him.

It is easy for me to take a clear position when I am personally invited by Father Friedrich to participate as one of the leaders at the coming retreat for young adults at the Münsterschwarzach Abbey. I am thrilled! Obviously, I would like to accompany spiritual songs on my guitar and speak about my personal experiences seeking God.

Back at the college, Ulrich overhears me discussing my surprise at the invitation with Humbert and Clemens after dinner. Unasked, he joins in our conversation – with his now-familiar gloomy look: »I don't know what you're up to, Christoph. You do realize that you have to ask Abbot Berthold for permission if you want to join them?«

»Oh,« I reply, taken aback. I had not thought that far ahead.

Humbert and Clemens exchange meaningful looks.

»Thank you for pointing that out, Ulrich. Next time I'm at Metten, I shall speak to the Abbot about it.«

I hope I sounded reasonably confident. I do not want to let it show how much my anticipation has been dampened. Abbot Berthold appreciates me, however, so I can be quite sure of his approval.

An unexpected headwind comes from a completely different direction. The novice master from Münsterschwarzach makes a special trip to come see me for a confidential conversation.

In my room, he cancels without hesitation my planned participation in the youth event: »Brother Christoph, it is not possible for you to participate in the retreat with us, as Father Friedrich intended. You are from Metten Abbey. Not Münsterschwarzach. Father Frederick seems to have gone off course when he invited you. Please forgive Father Friedrich's inattention.«

And then he is gone.

I am left alone and feel like I have just been hit in the head. Could such a thing be possible? What happened to the cosmopolitan warmth that surrounded me for the last year? I have always felt welcome in the company of the Münsterschwarzach monks; I believed that I was allowed to grow in their midst. And now, some red line is suddenly drawn to exclude me.

»After all, there are rules – and they apply to you too!« In the novice master's brusque rejection, I heard an echo of my father. Must I again prove my subservience?

Though I try not to let myself be defeated, I feel like I am failing. The rejection from Münsterschwarzach really gets on my nerves. I never expected such a blow. Moreover, despite all the hustle and bustle and new activities, I still have not succeeded in overcoming my inner emptiness. Nothing fills me lastingly, no matter what I try out.

What really nourishes my soul? I never seem to be able to find the answer. Dissatisfaction gnaws at me. It constantly eats its way through my thoughts, disturbs my sleep, and robs me of inner peace so that I feel exhausted and burned out. Meanwhile, I can no longer block out the pain of my ›inner wound«.

It can't be that now everything starts all over again – like at the beginning of my time in Würzburg, I write desperately in my diary at the end of 1982. Moreover, I don't feel as supported by my friends as I would like.

Not every problem can be solved with a smart book, reads a snappy comment in my notes because Albins ever-forthcoming book recommendations were getting on my nerves.

As I stare at the ceiling in the dark on another sleepless night, my inner voice speaks out: »Seek out a conversation with the spiritual director again,« it says. This is probably the most obvious solution. If my past seems to be repeating itself, then this would be the next step.

Unfortunately, Father Claudius gave up the office of spiritual director when an above-average number of new students enrolled at the college, and his duties as director of the institution took his full attention. So now I present my dilemma to Father Burkard, who seems a bit remote. He looks at me to examine but didn't say a word, and I was not sure if he understood my problem.

»You have neglected to take care of the originating life force of the primordial ground, of your Chi,« he finally states calmly.

I think I misheard.

»What's that?«

»Too much of your life energy has been channeled into your projects and activities for too long without you having taken the time to reabsorb the same level of vital energy. Your batteries are dead, Christoph.«

»What am I supposed to do? Nothing helps me.«

»Try visiting Father Anton. Perhaps your energy storage system needs the stillness of meditation to reboot.«

Seriously? What will the others – my friends, Ulrich – think of me then? Cautiously I paraphrase my concerns: »But you already know that his novel practices and doctrines are not without controversy?«

Father Burkard doesn't seem to be unsettled by this objection either.

»Dear Christoph, form your own opinion instead of being influenced by the prejudices of others.«

His soft voice sounds almost hypnotic.

»Your path should, by all means, lead you to where your source of strength is located. And you're the only one who knows when it has reached that place. Don't let other people clip your wings.«

He nods meaningfully.

I intuitively know he is right. Father Claudius's advice had once set the course for positive experiences in new directions. This time would surely be the same.

Unfortunately, my first experience meditating is disappointing; I do not feel like a new person at all when I leave the room that temporarily serves as a Zendo until Father Anton's new facility is finished.

At first, I did not feel anything, which is exactly what Father Anton predicted at the beginning: Without extreme discipline and even harder work, we would achieve nothing in Zen. The path is long and rocky. Hard, just as Father Anton is hard. It seems impossible to establish a human closeness to him. But maybe that is not meant to be. He is very clear about what he wants from us.

It is what we are all striving for: Inner clarity, a clarity to the point of complete transparency and emptiness, to accept God into us.

So I guess it makes sense. At least, I think I do.

I have not told the others for now. I do not feel obliged to reveal or to account for myself. After all, something new is beginning to happen: Gradually, the meditation exercises have become the most important thing to me. To simply follow my breath with all my attention, to let go of all emotions, thoughts, and impulses of the will, and to immerse myself completely in the moment has now become my life.

As a result, I have less and less time for Humbert and Clemens. When I skip a discussion evening with Albin, he confronts me in my small attic room: »What's going on with you, Christoph?«

His inquisitorial question disturbs me.

»Why, what's wrong?« I boldly answer with a question.

»I don't know what you expect from the hours you spend under Father Anton's supervision, but his method of contemplative immersion is certainly not the right path to self-realization.«

Deeply hurt, I can hardly contain myself. »Would you please let me organize my own free time? Besides that: Whatever happened to the idea of ›supporting every person in their being, regardless of their inner place?‹. Doesn't your reform pedagogical truth apply to me anymore?«

»More than ever, Christoph. That's why I'm here. Out of concern. It's ill-advised to follow a man who may cover his own insecurities with the exaggerated role of a Zen master and who tends to dismantle his students instead of fostering the master in them, as Gerda Alexander wishes.«

That's the height of it. If you're in a glasshouse, stay away from rocks.

»Now I know where your compulsive need to impose your worldview on us comes from. What complex are you compensating for? By the way, Matthew 7, verses 3-5, gives very clear answers about the nature of criticism – that is, about yourself, Albin,« I say.

»Oh, Christoph, what is this now? Do I have to refer you to Matthew 7, verse 15? Who is hiding in sheep's clothing? False prophets!« Albin counters, visibly annoyed.

»How do you measure a man except by his deeds? In this case, it is by the inner resonance of contemplation that Father Anton teaches me. I feel how deeply silent meditation reaches and transforms me.«

»Exactly, Christoph. Anton's influence reaches deep. How radical is the transformation his teachings require of you?«

Albin speaks to me insistently. He leans forward on his chair as if trying to reach me better.

»What's radical about turning off your mind? It is also part of deep Christian prayer.«

»Anton is not praying with you. He is practicing here 'the return to the authentic practice and experience of Buddha'. Under a Catholic roof! As if there's an overlap between Buddhism and the Catholic Church. Buddhism doesn't even recognize a Creator God!«

»Emilio Emomiya-Lassalle, who even as a priest and Zen master advised the Second Vatican Council, as I'm sure you know, he talked about 'Christian Zen' as we empty our minds in order to experience unity with God. Moreover, this Unio Mystica unites the religions and does not separate them. And that is the mystical experience I want to have.«

No sooner is the sentence completed than I can practically see Albin's next words. He is bursting with zeal.

»Oh, Christoph, if only you had said something earlier. What you lack is the enlightening reading of important mystics from the history of the Christian church: Master Eckart and Dionysius Areopagita are a good place to start. I'll bring you two or three books.«

There it is again: Albin's patronage.

»Not now, Albin. Really not now. I don't want to read. I don't find my need for deep inner fulfillment in books, no matter how important they are. I have tried so many things: Bible study, choir practice, Eucharist, adoration, and eutony. It's all too little. It is meditation that will cure me of my inner restlessness and my spiritual pain.«

I underline my words with energetic gestures. As clearly as possible, I try to convey my position to Albin.

»Even if the methods of Zen seem draconian – of course, my bones ache from sitting so much – I recognize in it the path that is intended for me. Please accept this. One more thing: I trust Father Anton completely. He's a visionary to me.«

Like Albin, I have leaned forward. I look at him firmly and

hope he has finally understood.

In vain. My friend just looks forgiving. »Okay, but remember that a lot is projected onto Anton, making him seem like he is automatically someone.«

I'm sick of hearing it. Impulsively, I get up and open the door for him. Reluctantly, he gets up, too. With two steps, he is next to me and says with extreme seriousness: »What I want to say is that I hope you are not deluded.«

»Don't worry, that's not going to happen,« I say quickly, and with confidence, wish him a very pleasant evening.

I simply cannot believe it: First, the rejection of the representative from Münsterschwarzach and now Albin stabbing me in the back. What about the ›colorful sheep‹ who, according to Clemens, are also supposed to be welcome? In the end, I was right, of course: As soon as I show myself as I am, it's not so easy for others to accept me. Even the Münsterschwarzach monks' ideal of tolerance does not accept everyone.

It doesn't matter. In 1983 I displayed my anti-authoritarianism and express my individuality – in public. For none of the young Münsterschwarzach monks can bring themselves to take part in the inauguration ceremony for the House of St. Benedict, despite the blessing given by Abbot Andreas. I willingly jump in and take over the honorable task of swinging the holy water vessel.

I also put my studies on side and prefer to spend my time in Father Anton's meditation house. Only in silent meditation can I fulfill my wish to reconnect with the primordial ground and heal the spiritual wound that has accompanied me since childhood. For me, the longing for a mystical experience of God leads only to the house of St. Benedict.

At the end of the year, a new star rises in my sky. Amatus, a new student now lives in the cell next to me. He is a year older than me. Not only does he look beautiful with his black hair and light beard, but he is also smart, funny, and popular. His charismatic personality makes him adorable, and I am instantly attracted to him. The way he talks, moves, throws his head back when he laughs ... all this makes my heart beat faster. Around him, however, I usually remain quiet because his sheer presence and warmth leave me speechless. It would never occur to me to open up to him, to talk about my inner abyss. My infatuation takes place in my head and chest – right next to my jealousy. Our walls are thin, and it is very animated when he has visitors. And he often has visitors. More often than I would like.

In the summer of 1984, I sat at my desk on a hot day and was unable to concentrate. I wanted to catch up on long overdue diary entries, but I could not write a single line. The voices from next door throw me completely out of focus, like an undertow. Just knowing that he is next door. That laughter – that is not for me. I wonder who he is with. Gregor, maybe? He is always interfering. It is unbearable. And it is so hot in here under the roof. If I open the window now, it will be even warmer. And I will hear even more from next door because Amatus' window is always open.

Hold on! Did the door just close? Are footsteps in the hallway receding? Only one person, by the sound of it. That means that he is still next door – alone. It is now or never.

As if pulled by strings, I leave my room to knock on his door.

»Deo?«

That voice. It is hard to breathe. Carefully I push the door handle down and enter his room without looking at him.

As the monastic procedure dictates, I answer, »Gratias.«

I can hardly speak. I close the door especially carefully. I must buy some time until I know what to say. Why am I here? What excuse can I make up? At some point, I must confront him. I look at him, sitting at his desk – more beautiful than ever. The sun's rays shone down on his head like a halo.

»Yes, Christoph?«

How open and friendly he is. Clueless, too. He knows nothing of my emotional distress. Well, what now?

My knees are getting weak. I need to brace myself. I cannot seem to find any words.

Frightened, Amatus jumps up and steadies me.

»Are you not well? You're very pale. Come and sit down.«

He drags me to the bed.

»Yes, the heat, of course. It's bothering us all,« he says

I nod weakly, unable to think straight.

»Would you like some water?«

Without waiting for an answer, he takes his filled water glass from the desk, presses it into my hand, and sits down next to me. So close that our knees touch. I feel even warmer. At the same time, goosebumps crawl over my body, and my mouth is dry as dust. I drink – very slowly because I must try to sort out my thoughts. It does not work.

Helplessly I sit with the empty glass in my hand next to the most exciting man I know, and I do not know what to do. He smells so incredibly good, too. I take a deep breath, and inhale his scent, which confuses my senses even more.

Amatus takes the initiative and puts the glass next to him on the floor.

»Feeling any better?«

His voice is close to my ear. I shiver as he puts one hand around my shoulder and the other touches my thigh. I cannot help but turn to him. His lips are so soft, his kiss so seductive – more erotic than any fantasy. Never before have I felt such a need to let myself go, to give myself up, to just follow the flow of my emotions. I just want to give myself to Amatus. Intuitively I respond to his touches, follow his example, and give him the pleasure I feel. As if we were one.

»I have to go!«

Suddenly I jump up from the bed and collect my scattered clothes.

»Christoph!«

Amatus has sat up in bed.

»What are you doing? You can stay.«

I look at him and stagger. His skin, his beautiful body, which I want to touch over and over again.

»No, I can't. I have to... study the scriptures.«

I get dressed as fast as I can.

»Oh, that's a pity. I thought we were going to spend the evening together.«

Do I hear longing in his voice? At the very least, I can make out desire. I find myself undoing my jeans button again.

»Christoph!« a better self calls me to order.

»I'm sorry. I have to go right now. I'll see you.«

In no time at all, I slipped out the door and into my room

a few meters away. As soon as I am safely inside, I lean against the door. I cannot take another step. My heart is pounding so loudly that my ears are ringing, and my throat is tight. Suddenly, my legs do not want to carry me anymore. I break down sobbing without restraint. Amatus can probably hear me through the thin wall. I do not care.

The next day I have to see Father Burkard as an emergency. I need immediate spiritual help to cope with yesterday's events. I broke my vows to the order! What's more, with a man. I'll never get rid of this double guilt. How can I go on with my life? Can I stay a monk? And what will my parents say if I must leave the monastery? My father, who always knew everything beforehand. Was he not right? I have failed!

What will become of my love for God? My worst nightmare seems to have become a reality.

To make matters worse, I meet Amatus as I wait impatiently outside the spiritual director's office for my appointment. As I pass by, he touches my arm fleetingly, as if by chance, and winks at me. I wish I could sink into the ground. Or rip his habit off at once. But I just turn red and lower my eyes. His confidence is enviable. He will manage to go on without a counseling session.

Or maybe he already had one a long time ago and is simply doing what he was advised to, I think, as I leave Father

Burkard's office after a much too short conversation, now completely upset. In retrospect, it seems absurd to me that I ever thought this spiritual director was unworldly. If anyone knows what is going on, it is Father Bukard. He has an enviable overview.

And, miraculously, from this viewpoint, he sees neither errors nor confusion nor mistakes. Obstacles or risks simply do not exist: »This sexual experience was, of course, not an accident. On the contrary, dear Christoph: You have experienced the immediate consequence of consistent, intensive meditation. It awakens the forces slumbering within you and sets them free. Your sexuality is part of it.«

I had thought a lot of things were possible – just not the surprising turn in the expected course of action that ran through his daring advice. I had expected the worst. Not with the suggestion »to consciously enter into a closer relationship with Amatus.« After all, we were »both in the three-year trial phase.« ›Trial‹ would mean trying life. If I wanted to keep »uncompromisingly to the temporal vow of chastity,« I should move to another room.

Is Celibacy only a possible option? As an alternative to a relationship – with a brother? I had not yet been able to consider this advice before Father Burkard was already giving me his ultimate guidance for my daily meditation routine:

»Whatever you decide ... whenever you meditate in silence, imagine how your energy spreads from your pelvis into your upper body, head and arms, and also into your thighs, legs, and feet. Open every cell of your body to your sexual power and let it spread like warmth throughout your body. Surrender your whole body to the sexual power.«

This is the most incredible thing I have ever heard. So I do not receive any blame at all; I have merely freed myself? Is that what he is saying? And sexual energy is like warmth circulating through my body – in meditation?

Now I should turn to Albin to see what he has to say about it, but our relationship is still tense and perhaps not yet resilient enough for a discussion of such bold propositions. I am also still alienated from Clemens and Humbert. Thus, I must see how I will get by on my own.

Because I do not know any other solution and because Father Burkard was once so right to recommend meditation to me, I trust him again. From now on, I will immerse myself in meditation, sweating my energy through all the pores of my body. The struggle rages most fiercely inside me when I sit at my meditation place during a group exercise and, at the same time, hear Amatus's warm laughter outside and how the other brothers join in. I want to cry; the struggle is so strong within me.

After an open conversation with Amatus – which makes me so ashamed that I even have to hide it from my diary – I change rooms. Far from his room, to the opposite end of the house.

Unfortunately, it is not far enough to put him out of my mind. Especially since we keep running into each other every day. Every time I meet him, I long for him. When our eyes meet, the world stands still for me.

I know it is not like that for him. He does not like to commit himself. He prefers to show off his independence and throw me into a roller coaster of emotions. One day, I am blown away by his suggestiveness: »See you later, Christoph?«

The next day I am in crisis because he will not look at me. Not a day goes by when he makes me forget what he said to me the first time we spoke: »You should not always take everything so personally, Christoph. Of course, I like you just as I like people in general. Men. Women. Exciting moments. They often just happen, out of the moment, out of a mood. I'm open to that. And I want to stay that way.«

These are the words that not only remind me how the world really works but also immediately send me back to contemplation. Without it, I have no idea how to return to my inner center, which waits for me at the back of my circling thoughts. Only here do I find access to my healing self-power.

Chapter 4: Enlightenment

In this state of mind, I return to my home monastery. The summer semester is over, and a groundbreaking decision is expected from me later this summer. Under other circumstances, it would be easy for me. But now?

After the confusing experiences of the past months, it is far from clear to me how I can make the eternal vows. But my monastic career leaves no other option: This is the moment to ask Abbot Berthold for permission to live as a monk forever. Forever celibate. Without a doubt, I will follow the call that I have always considered my vocation: to serve God. But under these circumstances, may I still receive the signs of profession, the ›Cowl‹ and ›Breviary‹ from the abbot and swear ›Stability‹ during this most sacred ceremony? Am I still worthy of the honor of living permanently at the Metten Monastery?

I have no idea how all the parts are supposed to fit together. Nor do I know how I can live an authentic life. I miss what I experienced in Würzburg: how like the Münsterschwarzach monks, I could share the most private feelings with my brothers in a completely informal way. Here I cannot talk to anyone about my personal struggle and doubts. Nobody here knows what happened in Würzburg. Sexuality is certainly not a topic that I could discuss with anyone here. We in Metten are different, and committed to tradition. And that is how I must be now. Adapted. Swimming with the current.

I would really like more time to think things over. But how can I explain myself to the abbot, who knows me as a kind and irreproachable young monk? I had four years to prepare. Why would that not be enough?

Because I fell in love, and my sexual – no, homosexual – desire is incompatible with my love for God. Nor do I know how lifelong abstinence is supposed to work in such circumstances. If I tell the truth, Abbot Berthold will immediately know that I am not a suitable candidate. And what, then? What are my prospects? I try not to think about my parents. It all seems quite horrifying.

Isolated in my monastery cell, alone with my diary and my dull thoughts, I imagine what it would be like if I belonged to the Münsterschwarzach Abbey, where I would not be left on my own. There, the abbey's new abbot has divided the monastic community into small groups called ›deanships‹, from which a spokesman, a ›dean‹, is appointed, who consults with the abbot about the individual members.

I like the idea of the abbot keeping an eye on each individual brother by hearing from the deans what is going on in the group, who has problems, or where support is needed. In this way, Abbot Andreas can fulfill his spiritual task to a greater extent than Abbot Berthold in Metten, who has no idea how little I still believe in my destiny. There are even said to be meetings in the deanships where everything can be said without reservation. One is given space to speak freely without fear of consequences.

Could such a progressive concept ever find a home in Metten? In my mind, I can already hear Ulrich saying: »I don't see anything wrong with staying with the tried and true methods. Group dynamics is just another flash in the pan that will never reach Metten.«

I suspect he is right. Things have been happening the same way around here for centuries; it is no wonder Metten feels stuffy and out-of-date.

If only I were in Würzburg – preferably in the room next to Amatus – and could breathe in that incredible openness and liveliness again, and participate in the extraordinary liberalness, even in my thoughts. I wish my brothers would show me Münsterschwarzach kindness: the feeling that in my need, I am seen and am not condemned for my views.

But these are figments of my imagination. Instead, I find myself alone and isolated because I can anticipate the turmoil I would provoke if I confessed. So I pretend that everything is fine. In the presence of my fellow monks, I perform the role of the carefree and striving young monk. That I blindly follow the same rigid agenda as they do makes me appear obedient. They have no idea how much strength this charade costs me.

Otherwise, I try to spend as much time as possible alone. I use every free minute to retreat to my own room to take a seat on my cushion in contemplative meditation. It is all that I have; without it, I would probably lose my mind. For the time being, my only friends seem to be meditation and my diary.

And maybe Wunibald, the economic administrator.

»Would you like to come over to my place tonight?« How familiar this phrase sounds – and what desire I associate with it. Involuntarily I break out in a sweat. But of course, it is not Amatus who stands before me after dinner, but Father Wunibald, who has been watching me attentively since my return. Did his humanitarian interest in his brothers tell him that not everything is in order with me? Nevertheless, his invitation surprises me. Apart from a few hikes and ski trips, we have never spent much time together.

»Yes, with pleasure,« I say honestly, with conviction. I look forward to hopefully taking my mind off things tonight.

In the corridor outside, I hear a jumble of cheerful voices coming from the rooms of the economic administrator's office. Oh no, not that! I had assumed that we would be on our own.

It will be impossible to speak confidentially with all this

noise. I think I would really rather go back to my room.

But oh well, so it is. I am here now.

»Hello!«

Cheerfully I enter the large office with its ample seating and greet the surprisingly large group of people there.

»Christoph, glad you're here.«

Wunibald hurries up and gives me a mug of beer.

»We haven't seen each other for ages. I can't wait to hear what you have been up to. How have you been?«

» All good. I've been going to some really interesting seminars.« My go-to answer works here too.

»Tell me, what's it like at the college? It's under the jurisdiction of the Münsterschwarzach monastery, right?«

»Hm,« I mumble. I sense the ice is getting thinner.

Wunibald seems not to notice my tenseness.

»Tell me, is it really so wild over there?«

His choice of words gives me my answer: »Wild?‹ I don't know what you mean. They are monks, after all!«

It is surprising how easily this excuse escapes my lips.

»Sure, I know.«

He lowers his voice and approaches me even closer: »It's only that compared to us, they are supposed to be open to all kinds of new and untested things, so we hear. Did you not get that sense?«

Instinctively, I take a step back. He has quite a penetrating way of getting to the bottom of things. Although we are talking out of earshot of the brothers, and no one seems to pay us any special attention, I imagine that I feel their nosy looks on my back.

»Oh, well, there are fewer prayer times,« I answer as naively as possible. I am hoping that a neutral answer will dampen Wunibald's interest. I am wrong.

»I heard from Ulrich that Father Anton is now in Würzburg and has his own house of meditation. Is it true that you were at the opening?«

I nod in silence. Stealthily I look around to see who else is present.

»Come on, don't make me drag it out of you,« Wunibald presses me.

»What's there to tell? Someone was missing, so I jumped in to carry the holy water.«

My voice sounds as angry as I feel. If only I had rejected this invitation.

»Oh, I see; Ulrich's story sounded more dramatic. As if you were under some sinister Münsterschwarzach influence.«

Why is he looking at me so strangely? Does he know something? What is it? Never mind. Just deny everything for now.

»What influence? I don't know what you're talking about, Wunibald.«

Do not let on to anything right now. Everything is perfectly fine: »I don't know what makes Ulrich think so. He lives quite far away in the house and is studying to become a teacher, so I don't really have much contact with him.«

»Maybe that's the problem.«

»What problem?«

What's this all about? I've never known Wunibald to be so insistent.

»There is no problem, like I just told you,« I say.

»You spend too little time with Ulrich and too much with the Münsterschwarzach monks, so I've heard. It doesn't come across well.«

I press my lips together and try to suppress my anger. Why does everyone think they have to tell me what to do? Before Albin, now Wunibald. And then there is Ulrich somewhere in the background.

Defiantly, I extend my chin. My father knew to interpret this gesture as a warning sign.

»No offense, Wunibald. I'm very sure I can manage to keep the balance. Besides, I know where my place is.«

Steely, I stand my ground without batting an eyelid. I almost believe my own daring lie. Finally, Wunibald gives in and lowers his gaze.

»Well, if that's the case.«

He hesitates for a moment before raising his head again.

»I just thought I should tell you myself. And since you seem so introverted since you came back and don't seem to let anyone get close to you, I thought it would be a good idea to invite you today.«

He laughs and says sheepishly, »So you can get back together with your brothers.«

I immediately seize this chance to escape the unpleasant situation: »That's why I'm going to see Barnabas. I haven't had a chance to have more than a few words with him yet.«

I leave Wunibald and take a seat on the couch next to Barnabas. The babbling, shallow conversation calms my nerves. There are no ominous innuendos or indelicate questions. Mechanically I say the right thing and pretend to be interested in his anecdotes about everyday life in the monastery in Metten, which do not interest me in the slightest.

When Wunibald says goodbye to us all a short time later, I am more than happy. I wish only to be left alone and to meditate.

The next morning, I knew right away what I had to do. Was

it the fruitful meditation or the restorative sleep? I do not know. All that matters now is that I put my decision down on paper:

Dear Abbot, dear Confreres,

After four years examining life in the monastery, I wish to ask you to permit me to make solemn vows. I do this out of the experience of my own imperfection and weakness, and therefore I ask you for your strengthening prayer. May God bring what He has invested in me to growth and maturity, to perfection and holiness.

Metten, August 31, 1984

Br. Christoph Heining OSB

Handwritten letter in personal collection

The words are so honest and, at the same time, so carefully chosen that no one could doubt my intentions. They speak of the sincere humility of the virtuous monk. I am right; In a chapter meeting, the monk's council grants my request for perpetual vows.

I felt an unspeakable relief in having found the right way forward, as I had in 1980 when I decided to become a monk. In time I had again realized that there was only one direction I could take: to live as a monk and priest, faithful to my traditional home abbey Metten, my first love, among the monasteries.

In all circumstances, for better or for worse, in all times, even in those that I do not yet understand, I will be, remain, and live here as a monk. All I must do is hide my other self, adapt to expectations, and become who I have been called to be. Only then can I live a pious life in all humility.

Soon I will start thinking about which guests I would like to have present at the celebration of my Solemn Vows. I may invite sixty people. Certainly, my parents and siblings, aunts, uncles and cousins, and furthermore family friends and schoolmates whom I have fond memories of. I will also invite brothers from other monasteries.

I design the invitation cards myself by making a copy of a postcard by the artist Walter Habdank. For the image, I choose a woodcut with the title ›In manibus tuis‹ as a motif› Being in your Hands‹. How beautiful that sounds! How beautiful it must be. To be safe and secure in God's hands. How beautiful it is to be held securely and at the same time tenderly – by a man. By that man, that one man, who seems to exist only for me. It is incredible that I cannot forget him, that he appears to me everywhere. I must invite him, of course. What would such an event be without him? And I would very much like to have Albin, Clemens, and Humbert there too. Even if our bonds of friendship are no longer so close, I am still aware of how they helped me find my way in my new life in Würzburg.

At the thought of seeing these friends again, I feel pleasantly elated and optimistic.

In preparation for the solemn vows, several days of the retreat are planned for me and Brother Rhabanus, during which we should be able to hear God speak to us. The vows are not an extension of daily monastic life but require special preparation instead. On the Sunday before the celebration, we are released from our duties to the community – as cantor during choir prayers, server at meals, or guide during the daily library opening. We are not allowed to be spoken to by priests or other brothers. We must cease to participate in recreation between supper and the night prayers in order to retreat into the silence of our own cell. We participate in the daily life of the monastery in silence.

To reflect by myself in this extraordinary way also means again being confronted with the fear of failure. Instead of listening in silence to the message God reveals to me, my mind is occupied by gnawing doubts about my suitability. Will I be able to renounce sexuality for the rest of my life? To suppress what sensuality means to me? My dreams make it impossible to forget how I feel. My feelings for Amatus are as present as ever. Everything has remained as it was, despite my heroic decision to take the sacred vows. More than ever, I long for a sign from God as to how I should live a virtuous life.

On top of that, we must also listen to Father Wilhelm's lectures twice a day.

Waiting for the assigned novice master to arrive in the novitiate and trienate's room together with Rhabanus is no fun either. We are totally different and have no real connection with each other.

In long-winded interpretations, the gruff Father Wilhelm prepares us for individual aspects of the solemn vows and explains in detail the Monastic Rule of St. Benedict. As he digresses again and again by sharing anecdotes from his own monastic days, I look out of the window into the monastery nursery and follow my own thoughts. I continue to meditate every day to control my inner tension. As soon as I emerge from meditation, my life once again seems abstract and gloomy, like a work of expressionist film art. Distorted perspectives and lurking shadows are everywhere. I do not know how much longer I will be able to withstand the pressure.

The handwritten document of my vows suffers from this extraordinary strain. In duplicate form, I must write down my commitment to obedience, to living a stable life, and to monastic conduct in beautiful handwriting. Time and again, I must start anew: sometimes, my hand trembles, and the writing is barely legible. Other times I think of the hours alone with

Amatus, lack the conviction that I am doing the right thing, and I no longer feel sincere about what I am writing.

Am I not deceiving all those who believe they see the irreproachable Benedictine in me? If I believe Wunibald, there are already those who doubt me, which makes it even more important to raise my head high and prove that they are wrong. Could it really be Ulrich who is behind this talk?

Well, he is the only brother who has seen me in Würzburg. Nevertheless, I find it difficult to believe Ulrich is malicious. I do not forget how he took care of me during my first visit and the composure with which he reacted to my confession at the Katholikentag in Berlin. I got to know him as a good man. Such a person does not engage in deceit.

Brother Wilhelm's stern voice calls me back to the present when he cites a passage from the Rule of Benedict, which we are to study before the next meeting.

Before taking the vows, the sacrament of confession is also required. As my confessor, I choose Father Jeremiah, whom I admire. He focused on group dynamics during his studies of social pedagogy, and now he applies the methods in his practical work at the boarding school, thereby making few friends among his confreres. Removing his habit, he plays football with the pupils in their free time, an affront to the strict rules. Modern spiritual songs are often sung as part of the mass he celebrates, and I like to accompany them on my guitar. The traditionalists among the Metten monks have little understanding of this ›bad habit.‹

»It's not possible that this nightmare, which some people glorify as a ›zeitgeist,‹ should replace organ playing. It was always good enough for us,« an elderly brother said mockingly the other day.

Jeremiah wants to change our monastery and the Catholic Church from within, and for this, he accepts numerous conflicts. I like his courage to swim consistently against the current. Somehow, I feel that I am on a similarly remote path, and I think I recognize a soulmate in him. For this reason, I wish to entrust him with the reasoning for my decision.

»If it hadn't been for that strange conversation with Wunibald, which served more to warn me than to hear what I had to say, I wouldn't have come a step further.«

I do not like to think back to that bad moment in my process of realization. Praise God; it is over.

»Looking back, I realize that Wunibald was hoping to reconcile the rumors about my life in Würzburg with my own story of the events – and he did it in his own special way.«

Jeremiah laughs a little at this point, and I cannot help but join him. Clear and direct is just foreign to Wunibald.

»At the very least, that conversation opened my eyes,« I

continue with determination.

»Because not everything I do in Würzburg goes unnoticed, it has been necessary for me to publicly commit myself to Metten and demonstrate loyalty to our monastery. It is something that I also feel deep inside. With God's help, I am sure I can grow up to be the essence of the monk I have seen myself as since my earliest youth.«

As I struggle to find the right words, Jeremiah looks as calm as Father Burkard. Who knows what has already been entrusted to him under the seal of confessional secrecy?

»You have made the right choice, even if it may have come about in a complicated way. It's the result that counts. I wouldn't give much credit to Ulrich's stories...«

I become very quiet. So now they are stories? What exactly does Ulrich know? Besides, I was in the triennial phase and was trying things out, so to be fair, I do not deserve any blame. Father Burkard had emphasized this point. And he is the spiritual director, so he must know. Besides, that is all finished and will not happen again. And the holy water – well, there will hardly be another dedication.

»... are you still listening to me, Christoph?«

From far away, Jeremiah's deep voice reaches my ear again.

»Don't overestimate Ulrich's behavior; I was just saying. He likes to make himself important. We know you, and I trust you.

I believe that there is a lot of potential in you and that you will fulfill the tasks ahead of you with God's blessing in an exemplary manner.«

Words fail me; I'm so moved. That's the kind of support I have longed for.

»God will make it right,« he says in conclusion. »He can write straight, even on crooked lines. Just have faith!«

I feel strengthened in my decision after this conversation, and I am sure that I have gained an important victory over my inner conflict. It is right that I vow to live as a monk for life because I can trust that God will give me the help I need to live under the Rule of St. Benedict. On October 28, 1984, it was finally time. The long-awaited ritual takes place in Metten's magnificent abbey church. In the pews, I see the expectant faces of Aunt Anna and Uncle Heiner, and my parents and siblings are, of course, also there. Friends from the past have also gathered, as well as church dignitaries from Cham and some student brothers from other monasteries.

Ah, how nice, Father Burkard came too. But – and I really can hardly believe it – nobody, really nobody from the Münsterschwarzach Abbey accepted my invitation. This is a blow I did not see coming. Sure, I have not heard from Amatus, Albin, Clemens, or Humbert lately. Yet I never took this silence for a refusal. Why should I? I believed we were friends – against all odds – and would accompany each other on our journeys.

Apparently not, I now realize. And that this disappointing realization hits me on my big day is, in principle, logical: Now I can definitively conclude my former life of trial and error and start forever a new life. Presumably, this is the lesson I should learn today – to no longer abandon myself to the worldly fickleness of my acquaintances but to rely on the power of God, which will always be with me. I deeply trust that all will be well under His protection as I solemnly approach the sunlit altar.

Only a few days later, I returned to Würzburg for the beginning of the winter semester. I greet the Münsterschwarzach monks in a friendly way, without any particular emotion. What was, is past. I am already much further in my thoughts because I am looking forward to a very special event. In the coming week, I will skip all activities at the university to spend five days attending a workshop on the subject of ›Prayer of the Heart and Dream Work‹ in the House of St. Benedict. Thankfully, Father Anton's recommendation allows me to participate free of charge.

Although I had already registered some time ago, it is only now, after the overwhelming drama of the celebration of my solemn vows – which returns to me in my dreams – that it is particularly exciting to explore my world from a different perspective. I have already experienced a profound perspective on my body with the Eutonic gaze. Now I am ready to open myself to the bottom of my soul.

Despite a large number of participants, the seminar leader and his assistant manage to create a very personal atmosphere. Individual consultations are offered frequently in order to work through the intense experiences of the course. A one-on-one conversation with Lejonidas August, in particular, leaves a formative impression on me. I have never met a character like this Swiss psychologist and meditation instructor. That is probably why I choose to open myself to him, hoping to benefit from his wealth of experience as he interprets the experience I received, taking my vows.

Alone, I have been unable to classify the troubling events: »I kneel before the high altar and must sing the verse of devotion three times. Without the help of the abbot and my fellow brothers, I would have failed. My voice did not obey me,« I say, recalling the agonizing moment.

»Suscipe me Domine, secundum eloquium tuum et vivam. Et ne confundas me ab expectatione mea. ›Take me, O Lord, according to your word, so will I live, and do not disappoint me in my hope.‹ The aspirant prays that the sacrifice offered – his life as it was, as it is, and as it will be – will be accepted by our Creator,« adds August, the trained theologian.

As then, I am again in tears. The memory of what I had borne in order to come so far had moved me deeply during the ceremony: Would my sacrifice be enough? Was I worthy of monastic life?

»I can hardly describe what was going on inside me. I had done as much as I could to be able to stand at the altar in all humility that day. From now on, I had to let things run their course – wherever HE would lead me. I feel my sexual desire – and I give it to God, my Lord. As if to say to Him: ›I give you who I am and how I am. Now, you do something with it.‹«

Tears run down my face.

»To cry is a sign of internal cleansing. So you should recognize that your life is already on a new course. Old things are now being washed away, leaving you and your soul. Your purification process is already in full swing. You are on the right path«, he says.

»Do you really believe that?« I pry a handkerchief from my pocket under the habit and blow my nose loudly. On the right track, me, of all people? You can't be serious. If he knew what I was really like inside, he would not say that. Of that, I am certain.

»I don't see any real progress yet. Since I took my vows, my dreams have become even more bizarre. Now there are no more differences. Instead, everything belongs, that is, both together. Do you understand?«

I am so confused that I am talking nonsense. August doesn't say anything but leaves me the space to sort my thoughts.

I try to gather myself and start again: »What I dream of is to merge into a mystical union with God. An inspiration that recently takes the form of explicitly sexual images. Me with men.« I hesitate because I do not want to be more specific.

»Do you understand what I mean?« I ask, tense.

August nods: »The Mandala image.« His tone is as matter-of-fact as these two words. It is impossible to tell what he is thinking.

I inhale sharply, close my eyes for a moment, and wish I were invisible. Or very far away. Far away from what has been the most embarrassing moment for me in a long time.

»We all saw it, Brother Christoph. I think most of us now have a picture of what it is that wants to express itself.«

That is right. Because I showed them. I even lifted up high, for the sake of better visibility, what I had painted with genuine dedication during the days of the course. A recurring image that will not let me go. Only when I interpreted this colorful mandala picture – in a black monk's robe – in front of the whole group did I realize what I was doing: presenting an explicitly phallic symbol that appeared as an extremely self-confident gesture.

»Right.«

I can barely hear my voice because thoughts of guilt and shame seem to drown everything out.

»It is a special test to reveal your inner self to strangers. As you may have noticed, others have found it difficult to imagine their dreams.«

He is right. I was not the only one surprised by their inner truth.

»That's exactly why we're here. To recognize together that your shadows don't only haunt you in your dreams, they darken your life, as well.«

That sounds wise, but it is not enough to comfort me.

» I'm sure that's right. But as an ordained monk, how am I supposed to deal with the fact that my imagination makes a connection between the experience of God and homosexual desire? This is not something I am supposed to talk about. And here I am holding up a picture!«

I can only shake my head at myself in disbelief and utter a loud sigh.

»I have followed God's call – all the way to abstinence and the commandment of obedience. There is no room for lust. I knew that. Yet nothing has improved. On the contrary: now spirituality and homosexuality are merging? This is absurd, and beyond any experience, I can think of. What I want to know is: How do I deal with it? How do I get my life back on track?«

»No matter how strange and odd they may seem to you, dream images are the messages of the unconscious. The analysis of your shadow will show which concrete archetypes have risen from the collective unconscious to deliver their messages in dreams and fears. We are expressly encouraged to interpret their symbolism. Only in this way can we find out what is really going on at the bottom of our soul.«

An explanation from the lecturer and therapy educator of the C.G. Jung Institute in Zurich. I am impressed.

»You have already experienced first-hand how your life as a monk is literally ›overshadowed‹ by tabooed ideas, repressed conflicts, and repressed sexuality. These shadows stand directly in the way of you becoming yourself.«

Is he offering a solution to my dilemma?

»We must now look at these shadows together, subjecting them to analysis, as I said earlier. Only then can we achieve a resolution of the inter-spiritual conflicts that have been caused by the shadows.«

That sounds like a plan. But is it applicable to my situation?

»Hm. But my problem is explicitly homosexuality. Doesn't that make a difference in the approach?«

For me, the difference seems significant.

»Sexuality overloaded with unconscious emotions is certainly one of your shadows. The orientation that you think you are following is merely another variation of the ways with which your sexuality is charged. Nothing more,« he patiently tells me, somewhat convoluted.

I am not sure I share that view. Maybe I just do not understand the relationships yet. I say nothing; I just keep listening.

»The goal is a release and liberation from all attachments such as desire, jealousy, exaggerated expectations, and so on. How can the liberation of the ego be achieved? Through withdrawal from the outer world. Through the Prayer of the Heart or also called ›The Hesychastic Path‹, we reach introspection and introversion. I often speak about the seven stages, which lead to individuation to the healed self, which was meant at the beginning of existence a priori by God. With the completion of the last step, you will have become one with your soul's primordial ground, the divine, and the world. For the individualized person, inner contradictions and divided personalities no longer exist. Undisturbed, they can devote themselves to their personal life-task for the benefit of the general public.«

»And that goes for me too? That's what my life could be like?«

I hardly dare to ask because the mental depression that I move through does not seem to fit with this sunny view.

»Absolutely! I can see the unconditional will to transform in you.«

He sounds quite enthusiastic, I think.

»The ›Hesychastic Path‹ is through the Heart Prayer, isn't it? It is, I believe, also a form of meditation.« Didn't Albin mention it?

»Right. A meditation that, through a recurring, simple prayer, is designed to bring about a self-confrontation in the struggle with the passions in a lonely inner place. Just as regularly as the heart beats, the same words of prayer are recited until they are synchronized with the heartbeat, and you pray involuntarily ›with the heart.‹ Your connection with God is then as continuous and steady as your heartbeat. It is essential. What burdens your ego in the outer life is not. Projections, passions, orientations, and the like can be let go.«

»These attachments do nothing for me,« I hear myself saying, lost in thought. In my mind, the pieces of the puzzle are slowly coming together.

»Do you know that I discovered meditation for myself because of a similar reason? Out of a mental burning that has accompanied me as my ›inner wound‹ since I can remember. It has not only forced me into religion but also into regularly retreating into silence when life outside overburdens me. In order to escape this pain permanently, I entered a monastery in the first place.«

I am not sure what to say next.

»Without any idea of the confrontation with myself that would await me,« I conclude, shocked.

»There is much potential in you, Brother Christoph. A real willingness to unite the contradictory parts of your personality. There is no other way. When the complete fragmentation of the emotional world emerges openly, you must have courage: If you don't courageously connect with your inner being, fatal ruptures will inevitably result. You have recognized this and have already taken action.«

In disbelief, I look at the man, and still, I do not want to believe it. I have had too many human disappointments recently, and I am growing more cautious.

»And you are sure you're talking about me?«

»There are only the two of us sitting here. Who else could I be referring to but you? Rest assured, I see you.«

It sounds like a promise. I am very quiet.

After a few minutes of silence together, I ask timidly: »May I tell you how my Solemn profession continued?«

»Go ahead, Christoph.«

»As the funeral bell rings to signal my renunciation from the old world, I lie stretched out on the floor, ready to surrender my life to Christ. At the culmination of the ceremony, brilliant sunlight falls on me and literally illuminates me. In all my life, I will never forget how I knelt before the altar with my arms crossed in front of my chest, not only feeling the sun on me but also being filled from within by a warmth I've never felt before. As if everything is infinite love in the light of HIS presence. This is what acceptance from God must feel like. The bliss cannot be described in words. To be allowed to experience this grace, to be seen by Him, to be meaningful to Him, is inconceivable. My awestruck amazement about the initiation experience continues to accompany me. It permeates my body and opens my consciousness of a new self. In deep devotion and gratitude, I have submitted myself to his will: ›O Lord, thy will be done.‹ I keep thinking about it because this wonderful conversation feels like the beginning of a new life.«

»That's quite possible. You are already in the process of going along the path of transformation intended for you in your new life. And – you already feel this too – it is not easy. Hard work awaits you. Transformation is painful. Long. And absolutely worth it.«

»Ever since Father Anton taught me Zen meditation, ›hard

work‹ has taken on a whole new meaning,« I let out. Frightened, I fall silent. Was I too blunt? I don't want August to think that I am not up to the task. Nevertheless, Father Anton's severity is notorious and often intimidates me.

»Father Anton is known for his extreme discipline. It has taken him far, and it's admirable,« August responds with a diplomacy I can only learn from.

»The Heart Prayer will be easier for you. To put fervor into it increases rather than counteracts its effect.«

I like what I hear, but sometimes I wish for a teacher who does not condemn emotions altogether.

»Intuitively, you already set out on the right path to clarification all by yourself. You have begun to deal with everything, not to sit on the sidelines, which makes you feel warm – in your sensations, in your thoughts, or in any other state of mind. You have revealed your emotions and fantasies and also shown what captures your consciousness. This will continue to drive you relentlessly and will make you run hot until your inner coherence is found. In the first stage, you will get to know your life fire. Your acquaintance with it you have described today.«

Chapter 5: In the Abyss

The fire of life burns bright within me. Its searing heat does not burn me but drives me on. It is the driving force on my own true path, my path to becoming a confident individual who is at peace with himself and the world. I am aware that it will take years before I arrive there. I am still at the very beginning of my spiritual purification.

I strictly abstain from sex and continue to practice letting my sexual power flow through my whole body as warming energy. This creates enormous resistance. Again and again, I break into tears or fear the nightmares that I spend the next day documenting. My ›self‹ is reluctant to let go of sexual desire. If I did not have the heart prayer to accompany me through the day, it would be difficult to get through it and achieve inner serenity.

Lejonidas had suggested that challenges would preclude a straight path. Overcoming them is supposed to make me stronger, not pull me down. I want to trust him, so I believe that this is how it will be. I am grateful that I missed a few university events to learn a valuable lesson for my life: »Change is possible – even for you!«

What a phenomenal prospect; weeks later, I am still looking forward to it on my journey home to Metten for the

Christmas holidays.

My main prospects show an orderly future, and a coherent life. Even professionally. After finally overcoming the hurdle of taking my vows, only the last two years of my theological studies and the deacon ordination separate me from the priesthood that follows. Then this long-cherished dream will finally be fulfilled. I look back with gratitude and satisfaction on a year in which I have achieved so much and in which I have succeeded so well.

A few days after my arrival, there was a knock at my door. Who might that be? I am not expecting visitors. The relationship with my brothers at Metten is by no means strong. It appears that the ›kiss of peace‹ that sealed my admission into their sacred community lies much further back than the celebration of my vows, which took place only in October. It seems to me that the meeting with Lejonidas has taken me a long way away from the monks in Metten. Who among them has comparable prospects?

»Deo?«

The door opens, and I am delighted to see this brother of all people. We have always gotten along well.

»Gracias,« Barnabas says.

Unusually official, he remains in the doorway and does not enter my cell.

»Abbot Berthold wants to see you.«

I am taken aback. This is unusual.

»I see. All right.«

What is this all about?

»Do you know what this is about?«

Barnabas shakes his head vigorously.

»And right now, please.«

I have never seen him so impersonal.

Is there anything else? What is he looking at? Is there something I should know?

»Good. So now you know.«

Without another word, he closes the door.

What strange behavior. Still, I see no real cause for concern. Have I done something wrong? No. Did not God himself speak to me during my profession? Would I have been able to have this profoundly touching and loving experience if HE had not accepted me? I feel confident when I approach Abbot Berthold in his office without suspicion. Surprised, I note his furrowed brow.

»Br. Christoph, after Fr. Ulrich came to visit me, I asked you here today. Can you guess what this is regarding?«

Intuitively, I answer as straightforwardly as possible. My head held high.

»No.«

Inside, however, I am on guard.

»It's about your spare time in Würzburg. Your visits to the House of St. Benedict, about how much, how very much time you spend with Father Anton, who calls himself a Zen Master. Above all, you neglect your studies, the real purpose of your being in Würzburg.«

With great effort, I prevent myself from expressing my amazement. Someone just pulled the rug out from under my feet with a powerful jerk.

I try to breathe calmly. But my heart is racing. What now?

»Is that correct?«

Seldom have I heard such severity in Abbot Berthold's voice. I don't know how to answer him. What he says is not untrue.

»It is correct that I take advantage of what the college offers in Würzburg. These include, of course, events in the House of St. Benedict, which, as you said, is under the direction of Father Anton.«

It is all true. I cannot lie to Abbot Berthold. At the same time, I must think about myself.

»How often?«

»What do you mean?«

I try to buy time while my mind races. What can I disclose?

»Brother Christoph! How often do you visit Father Anton's meditation center?«

An idea starts to take shape in my mind.

»As often as I realize that I need spiritual support to fulfill my duties. My yearning for God is powerful. In this way, I come closer to him.«

Abbot Berthold's expression confirms that I have hit the right note. But the conversation is not over yet.

»But why does it have to be meditation? What about Bible study and prayer? You're a Catholic monk, after all.«

Abbot Berthold's severity has given way to astonishment. A good sign, I think.

»So far, I have not yet succeeded in achieving this form of God's presence in self-formulated, independent prayer. That is why the ›Jesus prayer,‹ which I practice with the support of Father Anton, helps me. «

Not a word about meditation – too exotic for Abbot Berthold, who has spent his whole life in Metten's world of thought.

»And the ›Jesus Prayer‹ is, after all, part of the Christian tradition. I assumed you would be in agreement.«

He actually smiles. A faint smile, but still. In my mind, I pat myself on the back.

»Of course, I am familiar with the concept of the so-called ›Jesus Prayer‹ or ›Prayer of the heart.‹ After all, Father Gabriel from our neighbor, the Niederalteich Monastery, published ›The Pilgrim's Tale.‹ With it, pray without ceasing has gained some notoriety. Not that I practice it myself…« He raises his hands almost defensively, » … but I have read about it. So … you're giving it a try?«

He leans forward a little. Is there curiosity in his eyes?

»Just out of curiosity, what exactly are you doing? How does it work?«

I am more than glad to provide information if it will help me defend this subject that is important to me.

»It is about observing the breath and repeating the words ›Lord Jesus Christ‹ when breathing in and ›have mercy on me‹ when breathing out.«

Lejonidas explained it to me so simply back then. But I do not think it wise to mention his name now; no need to create more complications.

»I put my whole being into this ›peace of the heart prayer;‹ my feelings, my thoughts, my will. I concentrate completely on my breath. Whatever affects me recedes in time into the background, and I immerse myself in pure presence.«

Tense, I wait for the abbot's reaction. Will he be convinced by my explanation?

»Hm.« He rocks his head.

»In principle, there are no objections to this. The ›Jesus Prayer‹ is compatible with the Roman Catholic faith of the Western Church – despite its roots in the Orthodox Eastern Church. In Thessalonians 5, verse 17, the believer is requested to ›pray without ceasing.‹ That's precisely what you do, you said.«

Abbot Berthold nods and appears satisfied. It feels like a weight has been lifted from my chest.

» I take it you have no objection?«

»It means that I cannot approve if your studies suffer as a result of your undertakings.«

Abbot Berthold's gaze has darkened again.

»I understand that.«

I lower my eyes repentantly.

»I rely on your responsibility to live the life you have chosen. And that you will not, of course, betray the trust I have placed in you.«

The seriousness of his words gives me pause.

»Thank you,« I reply quietly.

Then I am released from the conversation and immediately flee to my monastery cell to understand what has been done to me. From Ulrich. That I thought was my friend. Which I wouldn't have thought in my life would betray me. I was quite convinced that Wunibald was trying to make himself important, and I did not take his warning seriously. What a fool I have been! I feel desperate. Once again, I find myself looking into an abyss. Just a moment ago, I wanted to embrace the whole world. Now I want nothing more to do with it, just to hide away and feel sorry for myself.

As I stand at my window and stare into the garden without seeing thinking about the conversation with Abbot Berthold. Although, thanks to Ulrich, I unexpectedly found myself in an ambush, I orientated myself quickly and reacted wisely. I offered Abbot Berthold a perspective that he could understand, and that was compatible with the image he had formed of me in recent years. One that whitewashed over what Ulrich had put in his head.

Ulrich – it all revolves around him. Who put me in this impossible situation? Ulrich. And what happens to him? Nothing, he is completely unharmed, always off the hook, while I must explain myself. Who confronts him?

I storm out of my monastery cell and head for his room. I am so enraged that I do not bother with politeness but open the door at once and ask my adversary the only question to which I cannot find an answer: »Why?«

Ulrich is typing on his typewriter and looks up in surprise.

»Why did you tell on me?« I confront him harshly.

»If you're going to barge in here, at least close the door and lower your voice when you want a conversation. Otherwise, close the door behind you when you leave.«

He continues to type, apparently unaffected.

I can hardly believe it! Of course, I will come in. I give the door a shove so that it closes with an unpleasant thud. I immediately resume my long-overdue »Why?«

Ulrich calmly types to the end of the page and pulls the paper out of the machine with a jerk. Anger is seething inside me; with the greatest effort, I hold myself back. If I overreact now, I will never find out anything.

»Why what? Why do I feel it is necessary to inform Abbot Berthold of your dereliction of duty?«

He looks up briefly, shaking his head. »Is that why you've come here? I don't believe it!«

He reaches for the next sheet and feeds it into the machine.

»You know, this question alone proves to me how right I was to point out to Abbot Berthold how you behave outside the monastery. As soon as the reins slip, you lose control and forget where your place is, what is proper and what is not.«

I am speechless. That hit home.

»In Würzburg, I saw who you really are. And I'm glad that I shared my concerns in this regard with our abbot. Now he can see the whole picture: You can't handle freedom. It does you no good.«

Paralyzed with horror, I listen to Ulrich talk. His icy cold words cut directly into my heart.

»I also let him know, of course, that I warned you, and tried to lead you back on the right path. I've tried several times to talk to your conscience. In vain, as we now know.«

Ulrich shrugs his shoulders.

»But it's not my fault. I did everything I could. You knew better, and now you have to live with the consequences.«

He turns away from me and flips through the papers on his desk.

Petrified, I look at the man in whom I find nothing of the sympathetic monk who many years ago acquainted me with the Metten monastery, to whom I opened myself so willingly.

But I cannot find this person in the person I have come looking for today. I don't recognize Ulrich anymore, bursting with 'righteousness' and complacency as he is. How could I have been so wrong? Now I am paying the price for my naivety. Is this really necessary? Must we end up like this? I should at least try to salvage what is possible.

»You better not say anything.«

Ulrich even succeeds in cutting off any meaningful word from me.

»I'm writing my Sunday sermon.«

To underline his words, he starts typing vigorously again. Without looking up, he adds: »And remember, Christoph: Please close the door from the outside when you leave.«

Shocked, I leave Ulrich's cell, carefully pulling the door closed.

A formerly deep and pioneering friendship has irrevocably come to an end.

Like a beaten dog, I sneak back to my cell. At least the way is short, so there is a good chance of not meeting anyone. I don't want to see anyone in this state.

Out of strength, I throw myself on the bed. I try hard to reconstruct the events of the last hour. First, the conversation with the abbot: His accusations hit me out of the blue. That he might have doubts about me naturally makes me worried. This was not what I wanted. I do not want him to think that I disobey him. I am merely trying to take steps in order to live up to my vocation and, at the same time, live in harmony with myself.

It may well be that the paths I have chosen do not appear straightforward enough to others. But nobody should doubt my deep love for God. For this reason, it was immensely important to help Abbot Berthold direct his focus to the decisive aspect: I would do anything to get as close to God as possible and become one with Jesus, even if that meant having Father Anton instruct me.

Would it have helped to tell the Abbot the whole story? Probably not. What does this good-hearted, but in my eyes, unfortunately rather an out-of-touch leader of the monastery know about the dark shadows hanging over my life? Would he be able to understand that these practices are actually my salvation and offer me valuable help in my life, without which I feel lost? Has he the faintest idea of what is going on inside of a soul and outside in the world? He entered the Metten abbey immediately after his studies. He has never had to prove himself outside the monastic community.

Compared to me, Abbot Berthold has probably never been compromised or even exposed to treason. Why does Ulrich have to study with me in Würzburg? Could he not have gone back to Salzburg? After all, Rhabanus studies somewhere else. If only Ulrich was not able to follow almost everything I do in real-time. Or if he knew what I no longer do and have let go. Who knows what he's been saying? Or could tell.

What if today was only the tip of the iceberg? How do I know what he could be up to next? It is he who is untrustworthy! I will never trust him again in my life, least of all, confide in him my deepest secrets. How do I arm myself against the next attack? Obviously, I cannot adapt my life to Ulrich's expectations. How would I feel without my meditation group? Without the therapeutic work with Lejonidas? Or without the Prayer of the Heart? It is inconceivable for me. For someone as small-minded as Ulrich, it is unimaginable.

Is Ulrich constantly put to the test? He must not fight my inner battles. In his position, it is easy to disparage other people and discredit a fellow brother. As arrogant and complacent as he has shown himself, I must reckon that he will not give up. He will not give up trying to put me in a bad light.

The question is: how will Abbot Berthold proceed? He is in agreement about the ›Jesus prayer.‹ Did he not also signal understanding in other ways? If I remember correctly, he said that my studies should not suffer from my ›activities.‹

Objectively I can say that it does not: I am satisfied with my grades. And he said that I should be aware of my ›responsibility.‹ I absolutely am.

That is why I use the ›esoteric paths of immersion:‹ to be able to follow the Benedictine rule and live a celibate life, to lead my life as a good monk.

I already feel better. From this perspective, viewed through a new framework, the recent events no longer seem quite so horrible. It is just a pity that I was unable to defend my interests in Ulrich's presence just as wisely and confidently. Instead, I let him make me look bad and scold me like a fool. But that will never happen again now that I know who I am dealing with.

With Lejonida's agreement, in 1985, I registered for six courses lasting several days to be led by him or his assistant. I give absolute priority to my personal development. In my opinion, the signs are only too good that I will now be able to make significant progress. I am finally in contact with a trustworthy spiritual guide who seems to know a way out of my misery.

Of course, it happens just as I had imagined: Ulrich feels called upon to report me again. Naturally, the next time I visit the monastery, I am again summoned to talk to the abbot. Am I uneasy? No. This time I know what to expect. I am prepared; I know what to say.

Abbot Berthold is different. He looks rather disillusioned.

»After our last conversation, I trusted your change of heart that you would give priority to your studies at the university.«

Now I hear from Ulrich that you regularly hideaway for nearly a week in Father Anton's meditation center instead of attending your courses. Once again, I have to ask you what you have to say about this.«

»Ulrich does not know what he is talking about. There's no conflict.«

I try not to let my sudden nervousness show. My self-confidence is dwindling under the abbot's critical gaze.

»That's not how I see it. In fact, there is a very concrete conflict between your official schedule and your other activities, Brother Christoph.«

I feel myself getting tense. I hope that I can at least find the right words: »Well, actually, it's like this: Objectively, there is no drop in my performance; my reports prove it. My grades are as good as ever.«

I ignore Abbot Berthold's raised eyebrows and just keep talking.

»It is especially important to me that you understand why this is: because for me, just like heartfelt prayer, the intensive retreats in the House of St. Benedict are a source from which I draw strength for my everyday life as a student. They help me to survive emotionally in the dark and lonely night and to not fall prey to dark forces.«

I fall silent.

Even the abbot is silent. He is impressed, I hope.

»It's best if I get a picture of this Mr. August for myself since you're already spending so much time with him. Then I can judge for myself whether he is trustworthy,« Abbott Berthold says.

This is exactly what I was hoping for. What a coincidence

that the abbot himself now had this thought.

»That's an excellent idea! Lejonidas August can explain this reciprocal relationship to you much better than I can. He is a self-studied theologian and leads the courses in the house of St. Benedict. In this way, you can experience firsthand what I really do in Würzburg.«

»That's what we'll do. It can't hurt to get to know each other,« he concludes.

An enormous weight has lifted from my chest. I need not be concerned that Abbot Berthold still seems cautious. Getting to know each other will reduce his prejudice as the abbot will understand that Lejonidas and the courses he offers are not a threat to my spiritual well-being and that my professional career is not in danger. I feel confident.

A few weeks later I drive Abbot Berthold to Würzburg. I am curious to see how the head of my monastery will get along with my star – my spiritual guide. Ideologically, different worlds are coming together: One, a representative of the institutional church, a man of God. The other, a trained theologian, Catholic, but specialized in counseling through analytical psychology and immersion practice.

As far as I can tell from where I am – I watch their ›summit meeting‹ from a distance – they seem to get along surprisingly well. As I had hoped, they seem to be on the same wavelength.

On the drive home, I am very pleased to hear words of such praise for the Swiss teacher, and it seems Abbot Berthold's fears have been unfounded. Wisely, further meetings have been arranged so that the thread of conversation does not get lost, and I can ›officially‹ continue to work on myself under Lejoida's guidance.

In effect, what this means to me is that what Ulrich says is irrelevant. The effect of his words should fizzle out in the future because the abbot now knows better than him what is going on. Once again, my life feels as if I have a free ride on an open road. I am free again to do what is good for me, what I need.

After this obstacle has been cleared out of the way, a perfectly straight path lies before me. Now I can concentrate on my thesis. As a subject, I take my seminar paper on dance and prayer from my foundation studies and raise it to a new level. As soon as I have my diploma in hand, the deacon ordination is imminent, followed only a few months later by ordination as a priest. Then my life's goal will finally be fulfilled. I can hardly wait.

I am so happy about these glowing prospects that the sparse contact with my fellow brothers does not bother me much. Rather, I direct my consciousness in everyday life to the act of breathing, allowing me to feel strength and salvation rather than my emotional conflict. During the evening recreation the informal get-togethers, I no longer seek their company and, conversely, am hardly ever invited. The differences between us have grown too large in the last few months.

My time in Würzburg has changed me a lot. It is now more important to me to maintain close contact with people who think like me. People by whom I feel understood because they are on an inner journey just as I am. In their presence, I do not have to pretend to be someone else. We know our own abysses; together, we can look into the dark depths and confront the shadows. They know my mandala image; I know their secrets. This creates an enormously strong connection, one that need not be broken by the fact that I must regularly return to my monastery in Metten. The new friends I made in Würzburg during Lejonida's seminars came to visit me at the monastery gate. There should be nothing wrong with it. This is the publicly accessible area to which even women have access. Just a visit. The other monks also have visitors.

It is completely incomprehensible to me why this is such a sharp thorn in my confreres' side that I am called to answer the abbot's questions a third time. This time I must explain what is happening on the monastery grounds.

»Who are they? What are the conversations with these

people about?«

Abbot Berthold's disappointment with my behavior is obvious. To have three crisis talks with the same monk in a relatively short time has probably never happened to him before.

I try my best to allay his concerns. Even though I am a little nervous, I remain confident. Twice already, I have succeeded in turning our talks in the right direction. Why not today?

»These are people who I met in the House of St. Benedict in Würzburg or who know of my interest in meditation. I meet to talk with them outside the monks' enclosure at the gate.« I laugh, embarrassed. Even to my ears, it sounds forced.

»And why do these people come to you? You're a monk, a student, not a priest they can confess to.« Abbot Berthold does not hide his lack of understanding.

»They know that I work hard on myself: dream work, bodywork, that sort of thing …«

I see him frown again. Not a good sign. I wipe my sweaty hands on my robes.

»… as I learned from Mr. August. These people trust me with a certain competence to look at their dream pictures or drawings and to recognize something. Then they visit me in Metten and talk about themselves.«

As soon as I finish the sentence, I regret it. For someone

like Abbot Berthold, to whom this kind of introspection is completely foreign, all this must sound completely nonsensical. His next question proves that he is really faced with an enigma: »And why do women come to you? Are they in love?«

No! Why should they? Was he not listening? It is a mental-spiritual development process. Christ dwells in me, in the depths of my soul, and wants to be born through me. That's the authenticity my friends and acquaintances long for. In this way, we are on a common path. I know that, and I wish that the abbot would understand it too. At the same time, I realize with growing despair that I do not know how to find the right words for the abbot. I do not know how I can break down my world of experience in a way that is understandable and plausible to him.

After a deep breath, I take off running again.

»We meet on a purely brotherly-sisterly level as companions, all of whom are on a path that confronts us with similar life challenges. It's, so to speak, kind of the same dimension of a spiritual growths process in which we are traveling.«

As soon as I finish the sentence, I feel that my emotional connection with the abbot has been severed. I bite my lips. If only I had kept my mouth shut after the first sentence. But the wonderful opportunity to get into conversation with all these different people always carries me away so I lose myself in terminology. This may be appropriate in conversation with like-minded people, but it drives a wedge between the abbot and me.

You can see I went too far. No one has ever spoken to him like that before. He has no need to voice his consternation; it is obvious. He does so anyway.

»Brother Christoph, I must tell you: I don't know you anymore. You are no longer the Armin who joined us before!«

His words strike me to the core. When he then sends me away with an energetic hand movement, I feel as if I have been sent into exile.

As usual, I know only one place of refuge: my monastery cell. It is equipped like no other in the building and destined as my place of power. In the middle is a meditation cushion for my daily meditation exercises as well as two icons from the Russian Orthodox tradition so that I can align my inner compass even here in this Roman Catholic monastery. Right now, I need all the spiritual help I can get in order to process what happened and to find answers.

Above all, I have no idea what consequences this conversation will have. Does it have to have any? What happens if I appeal to Abbot Berthold again – in a letter perhaps – in order to explain my point of view again? On the other hand, would it then look like I do not have the courage for an open conversation? One which I do not know that he would grant. We have already tried three times.

I am so worked up that I can hardly enter meditation. Even my heart's prayer does not reach me now. My thoughts circulate without a moment's rest. I am already considering another option: maybe it would be better to forget the matter for a while. Perhaps if I were more discreet? Maybe then the picture of the exemplary Brother Christoph, who is seen and loved everywhere, will come to the fore again?

In any case, I must now concentrate on writing my thesis to prove the truth: that heart prayer and silent meditation contribute to my good grades. I just want Abbot Berthold to see it the same way: That this daily practice does not distract me but rather strengthens me – in my everyday life as well as in my faith.

It also strengthens my belief that everything will be fine. When the monastery's Council of Seniors met in February 1986 to discuss my deacon ordination in April and the priest ordination three months later, I tried to await the decision as calmly as possible. There has been no further conversation with Abbot Berthold that might have caused me to worry. I know that I am deeply rooted in my faith and feel an equally unbreakable attachment to my home monastery, even if it is less liberal than other abbeys. My home is here.

I know that the abbot will personally inform me of the outcome of the conference. Therefore, it does not surprise me that Barnabas stops by my monastery cell shortly before noon: »A decision has been made. The abbot awaits you.«

And he is gone. I did not have a chance to ask him if he knew the outcome. I did not see anything; even his voice sounded indifferent, as so often lately. We do not get along with each other as well as we used to. It does not matter; it is what it is. It is more important now to focus on the conversation with the abbot. Even if I do not have to say much, he will simply tell me the date of the deacon ordination.

He will, will he not? I have never seen such seriousness in Abbot Berthold's face before. Formally, he asks me to sit at the large conference table made of solid oak.

I already feel weak in my knees. I am glad to sit down.

»I'll make this short, Brother Christoph. You have aroused enormous suspicion through your pastoral conversations at the monastery gate, which were without any church authority or assignment. I have just discussed the fundamental reservations about your ordination to the priesthood that have resulted from this with the elected representatives from the community of solemn professions. And we have come to the following unanimous conclusion: Your deacon and priest ordination will not take place this year. It will be suspended for one year.«

My throat feels like it is closed, I feel afraid I will not be able to breathe, and the pressure on my chest becomes almost unbearable. I am freezing cold.

Abbot Berthold continues abruptly: »Brother Christoph, we do not know what you are doing in your confessionals: whether you are forgiving people's sins or whether you are providing counseling.«

I do not say anything. I do not have any words. My head is completely empty.

»You may go.«

With difficulty, I rise, staggering. I clutch the back of the chair for a moment so as not to lose my balance. This turn of events far exceeds my comprehension. How I managed the long way to my monastery cell, I forgot as soon as I arrived there. I cannot go to lunch, as exhausted and dejected as I feel. I do not want to see anyone; I only want to be alone. Apart from that, I have no idea what to do, especially what might make me feel better now. Or how my life will go on. I am not sure where I stand now. Is it even possible to suspend the deacon ordination? Is there a precedent? I have no idea. Who am I now?

The lines in my diary are barely legible: thick tears dissolved the ink as if they wanted to wash away the last bit of me.

Lejonidas once said that crying was a good sign, that resistance dissolved, and that a transformation had begun.

Is that what is happening to me now? I have written my mentor repeatedly in the last few months. What can I tell him? He is a man who thinks so highly of me. Or has thought so highly of me. Who knows what he will think of me now?

What am I now? Failed. Nothing more. Everything I have longed for – will not happen. Putting off for a year is the same as ›not going to happen.‹ Which, in turn, means: ›you are unworthy of the priesthood.‹

Oh, how I fought to get this far, the things that I have taken upon myself. With determination, I wipe the tears from the paper and can no longer make out anything. What a symbol: as if I had never achieved anything. In the end, everything was in vain.

Even the discussions with Abbot Berthold. What did they bring? Nothing, absolutely nothing. He still does not understand that the conversations with my acquaintances are based on an analytical approach, not a pastoral one in the church sense. And nobody is in love with me. Why am I not allowed to sincerely want to help people from the bottom of my heart? How far away have I moved from my abbot if he no longer recognizes who I am? Why does he not know that I live a spiritual life from within? That I am a monk from the bottom of my heart and want to become a priest, nothing more? I do not question this existence but do everything to get the strength to be able to lead it according to the Rule of St. Benedict.

My tired eyes fall on a gleaming icon of Mary with the baby Jesus, which I love very much. She always helps me to get in touch with my feelings and, thus, to find inner clarity. Maybe she can give me the strength to understand what has just happened. If the external world is mercilessly out of control, then at least I am secure in my own little kingdom. Here I feel safe.

I feel isolated from my fellow brothers. They do not understand me and have no interest in putting themselves in my position. I have lost sight of any goal in life, any orientation.

The only ray of hope is going back to Würzburg for a few months to finish my last semester of studies in the summer of 1986. At school, my meditation group will give me reliable support and suggest something almost like a carefree time. However, I am already saddened by the fact that our paths will separate for the time being at the end of my studies. To signal goodwill, I plan to suspend the meetings at the monastery gate for the time being.

Despite this stressful, emotional situation, I at least manage to complete my thesis to my complete satisfaction in ›Growing for salvation. Towards an Experience of God – Revisited through Dance-Meditation‹, I show the practical connection between my religious education minor and my pastoral theology major. The special emphasis is on pastoral psychology.

»Far-fetched« and »esoteric fluff« are my brothers' harmless comments I hear whispered to each other when they think I cannot hear them. Abbot Berthold reacts in a similar negative way, even if he has nothing to criticize about the ›good‹ grade.

»I do not see any practical use in this work. The thematic connection to your personal interests is more than obvious,« he tells me dryly.

Instead of being allowed to hope for a calming of my overall situation – I have successfully completed my theology diploma, after all – I feel once again left out in the rain.

I do not seem to be doing much these days. I live from moment to moment, from choir prayer to choir prayer, from lunch to dinner, without tasks, without distraction, without encouragement from within the monastery walls, and without any significant contact with the outside world.

Abbot Berthold, who sees me for the time being as a rejected priest, ultimately finds a place for me for half a year in an uninspiring internship in Straubing. He is very impressed by the vision of the priest there to have the parish church elevated to a basilica and by his love and devotion to liturgy. So much so that he hopes he will be a good influence on me.

I am less enthusiastic. If I belonged to the Münsterschwarzach Abbey, I would have other opportunities. The monks there have more diverse choices, I think sullenly. Only my work with the youth, who I am directing in a musical, gives me as much pleasure as our exciting performance in the parish church. So much so that I am tempted to believe I have gained a foothold again and have succeeded in coming to terms with the circumstances of my new life. If only I was not reminded at the beginning of 1987 where my place is. Or where it is not. Once again.

»Brother Christoph, once again, I do not have better news for you.«

Why am I not surprised by Abbot Berthold's announcement? February has not been a good month for me for some time now. To be summoned to the abbot's office once again this month after another senior council meeting does not bode well. These were the omens of bad news last year. All that remains is for me to prepare myself for what is to come. I cannot do that either.

»We have not been able to form a different, better opinion

of you over the past year. We still do not trust you to properly exercise the priesthood and the sacrament of confession. It is with a heavy heart that we have decided to give ourselves another year to reflect.«

Abbot Berthold's face shows no emotion; he speaks objectively and is much too neutral. There is no sign of compassion to show me if he is concerned that my world might remain in shambles.

As if rooted to the ground, I sit in the uncomfortable visitor's chair, lacking the last ounce of energy to get up. I no longer feel anything; everything inside me seems numb.

»Brother Christoph? You may go.«

Abbot Berthold's cool voice barely gets through to me.

Go? Go where? Do I still deserve my monastery cell? Ordination, apparently not. No one mentions deacon ordination anymore. No one can associate me with church ministry anymore.

A light touch on my shoulder makes me jump up: »Brother Christoph, other meetings are coming up. Perhaps you would like to take the opportunity to go to your cell and pray?«

His words sound almost like mockery to me. For, of course, he does not mean the prayer of the heart of the Eastern Church but the discursive prayer that he himself practices, but which brings me little in these terrible days and nights. I cannot remember a single biblical passage that has brought me peace of mind in the last months.

Weeks later, I still cannot cope with this renewed rejection and humiliation. Even at my internship, I feel exposed and looked at critically. It is common knowledge that other graduates, after completing their studies, find themselves in a completely different place in life. Whereas I remain a nobody – which leaves a dubious impression. Even far away from Metten, I cannot get rid of the impression that people are talking about me behind my back.

At the end of the internship, I return to the emotionally cold wasteland of my monastery and clung tenaciously to my own daily schedule as if my life depended on it. Every morning at 4:15 a.m. I write down the memory of my dream. What the inner guidance from those dream images tries to tell me, I record during the day with crayons or in models made of clay. I am also no longer satisfied with the letters that I so diligently send to Lejonidas. Originally, I kept him informed of my progress. Now that I am going nowhere, my texts read strangely bloodless, I find. I long for enlightenment, but I cannot overcome the night-black darkness.

Things cannot go on like this. To make matters worse, the holiday season is coming up. The prospect of the last week of summer haphazardly dragging on, which simply cannot be surmounted by coursework with Lejonida's assistant, drives me crazy. As if I did not already have too little to do. My nagging dissatisfaction is reflected in my regular correspondence with my mentor.

As if he sensed my distress, for once, he replies immediately. Do not complain! Use the time wisely. Withdraw and entrust yourself to discover new inner paths. Face the shadow, for you cannot escape it. Trust in heavenly guidance. I knew right away what he meant; we had talked about it briefly before.

Following my intuition, I decided in August to rent a holiday apartment in a remote area of Baden to live like a hermit for the rest of the holiday. Behind closed shutters, nourishing myself fully but sparingly, completely focused on my spiritual goal: I face an intense confrontation with my loneliness.

With the decision to withdraw from the world, my search for the right answers will hopefully find its much-desired end. For me, this step presents the possibility of finding a solution to which I can devote myself completely.

I expect a tough struggle with my demons, but I count on the fact that the dense netting of ritualized actions that I voluntarily impose on myself will catch and carry me through.

5:00 Get up - morning wash

5:30 Tibetan health exercises (Kum Nye)

6:00 Three periods of twenty-five minutes each of upright, motionless sitting in silence, interrupted by slow, meditative walking

7:30 Morning praise (song and prayer)

7:45 Breakfast

8:15 Cleaning the meditation room and house

8:45 Break

9:30 Sitting upright in silence

10:00 Read: ›Talking with Angels‹

10:30 Three periods of twenty-five minutes each of upright sitting, interrupted by meditative walking

12:00 Lunch

12:20 Break

14:00 Three periods of twenty-five minutes each of upright sitting, interrupted by meditative walking

15:30 meditative walking in nature

16:15 Sitting upright in silence

16:45 Kum Nye exercises

17:15 Mood painting - sitting upright

18:15 dinner

Break

19:30 Three periods of twenty-five minutes of upright sitting, interrupted by meditative walking

21:00 Evening praise

21:45 Sleep

With courage, I plunge downriver into my stream of consciousness with the request for a revelation of my life's circumstances. I quickly notice how feelings and moods move inward, fueled by my burning interest to get on my own track.

Uncomfortable insights are already revealed during the second night in crushing dream images.

One of my brothers celebrates his First Mass as a priest in his home parish.

In the end, he gives the blessing of his First Mass; Children form a cordon, sing for him, and play the guitar. It should be me who receives this honor in his place. But I stand on the sidelines, watching from a distance, full of envy, invisible to those involved as if I do not exist. No one takes note of me. I wake up bewildered and sad.

My life has hit a wall. And now, this wall separates me from the world of those people who effortlessly achieve their professional goals without detours or obstacles. I stand alone. Thrown into isolation with myself. How could it have come to this?

During the meditative walking on the third day, a

realization comes to me from the furthest, most isolated corners of my consciousness: fantastic images full of lust overtake me with unexpected unrestrained. At first, I see myself again walking through the Bavarian woods on the way to Metten. Shortly afterwards, more than vivid scenes of being together with Amatus make my body shiver. And also what my one-time secret visit to a gay center in Würzburg triggered in me, I can hardly believe even now.

Could I hope for real understanding in the monastery of my first choice if I confided my inner struggle to my fellow brothers and the abbot? Would they understand why I cannot help but go my own way to reconcile my love for God with my sexual identity? On the other hand, I only become stranded when I have to hide my true nature, my inner core. I cannot be anyone but who I am. Sexually and spiritually.

On the fourth day, while painting, I wallow lustfully in the representation of my inner images and let them resonate in my entire body.

Some kind of transformation seems to be underway: »You don't need to be afraid of your sexuality. It's a direct path to your spirituality.«

Immediately I write down this message from the bottom of my soul. There is such promise in it, in which I simply want to believe – despite the adverse circumstances at Metten.

During the fifth night, my soaring ends with a sudden crash and the fear of another deep fall. In a frightening dream, I fall nearly uninhibited into a void. In vain, I try to hold on to an easel, but it bends under my weight and gives way. Then I try with all my might to crawl into a gap between the table and the ceiling. The table seems stable, but I fear it will give way under me. Where will I end up, then? Where am I supposed to go?

A girl in the dream knows the way out: the table is standing on a broad surface; I can free myself.

I suppose the message is that »old entanglements and fears must disappear so that there is room for new thinking.« When the fear of free fall is overcome once and for all, the world is open to me too.

I had a delightful experience the next day when I sat in silence. Suddenly I feel an unexpected energy flowing through me with a gentle tingling sensation. A deep humming accompanies this overwhelming experience.

In the course of the day, I am filled with Elysian melodies, and my mood brightens. In my mind, I see myself reconciled, dancing in the monastery's monks' choir amid my brothers.

»They will send me on, not wanting to keep me for themselves, once they realize what joy of life being close to me can bring!«

When I wake on the seventh and last day, I am not only

wrapped in sacred music but surrounded by a glistening bright aura. Literally radiant, I see myself approaching my neighbors, opening myself up to them willingly.

As a completely new person, I have finally found what is ›above,‹ at the highest point of my inner journey to the self.

On my way home by train, this quiet happiness continues to inspire me. How I spent a week just for myself reflected on my own being, carried by spiritual trust in inner order. Did this solitude lead me to deeper self-confidence?

I think so.

Right now, I am certain of it. Nevertheless, it remains to be seen how I will succeed in integrating the newly gained insights into my daily life.

I want to believe that I have understood my world because I discovered HIS plan for me. In a very simple way, actually: by going into strict introversion, without outside distractions, following only my own rules. In this way, I passed through seven different levels of my consciousness in seven days until I was rewarded with the prospect of an individualized personality.

Did not Lejonidas once talk about this very thing? That the path of change would also lead me to that very point where I would become aware of the core of my being, what kind of person I can be: Free from fear, unconcerned, but not careless.

Full of love for people. Awakened, enlightened, and reconciled with my environment.

I will then have left the former man with his earthly upheavals and capricious mood swings far behind me. I will no longer be a part of this world.

But for now, I still live in it, I realize immediately upon my return to the monastery. Nothing has changed here. Nobody asks me about my holiday experiences or seems to take notice of my return with interest. No brother comes to mind either, to whom I might share what has happened to me during the past seven days. Would anyone even want to listen? No one here wants to walk in my footsteps. For this reason, I find the same situation as when I left: Nobody recognizes me, recognizes who I am in my heart.

Otherwise, I would certainly be considered capable of more than the paltry five religious lessons I am supposed to give each week teaching the catechism. In a primary school! Unbelievable. How should I know how to handle children? I am rooted in the spiritual tradition of Zen meditation and the heart prayer, not in educational work. But I cannot complain: Additionally, two groups of altar boys have been assigned to me. My former fellow students celebrate the Mass – I lead children's groups.

Occasionally a silver lining appears with the beautiful name

Adelindis. We regularly get into conversation when this extremely likable woman brings or picks up her son at the class for the altar boys. Our deep common interest in meditation connects us. I have never met a person like her before, a single mother and dance therapist, and she practices something with energy work as well. I always look forward to the encounters with her in advance; there is a refreshing energy in them. I enjoy having this appreciative relationship in my immediate environment. This is balm for my soul, which I am so eager to develop.

Fate shakes me again; The Pastor of my home parish in Cham has come to find out what is wrong. »We're waiting for you. For two years, we have been hoping that you would celebrate your First Mass in your home parish. But nothing happens. Why?«

Even though he makes it short and sweet, his words hit me to the core. I hear an accusation, feel like I am on the defensive, and am overwhelmed. The right words to exonerate me and appear comprehensible to the Pastor do not come to me. I do not want to repeat the arguments of the abbot; they do not reflect my truth.

Fortunately, my Pastor does not wait for my answer at all but speaks in fury: »You are ready, aren't you? You have completed your studies – successfully, I know – you are an ambitious young man who wants to do God's work. So, an absolutely suitable candidate. Then what are you waiting for?«

Father Greindl, Father Ellinger's successor, shakes his head vigorously.
»I am puzzled by the decision. I don't know what's going on here.«

His sudden departure takes away the need for me to answer: »I will now speak to the abbot myself. After all, I made a promise to my parish. That is why I made an appointment with him,« he says and hurries out of my cell.

Oh no, not that! Pleadingly I looked at my Mary icon as if she could give me advice in this hopeless situation. What will he think now when the abbot tells him that he mistrusts me? I do not imagine that the priest will believe every word he says. But everything is different from what the abbot thinks.

Right now, I wish for something of the inner sovereignty and divine splendor that, only a few weeks ago, made me shine and was able to carry me through all my earthly hardships. On the contrary, I feel only utmost tension, as if I am on guard. The magic of my seventh day as a hermit seems to have been blotted out by the exhausting, inner struggle for survival within the walls of the monastery.

Father Greindl steps through my cell door for a second time, this time visibly shaken. I wish he would not say anything.

Then I could give in to the illusion that I still enjoy his trust — even if his facial expressions are speaking a different language.

Unfortunately, I am not spared: »Regrettably, I couldn't do anything for you. Not even for your hometown.« Never before have I seen such resignation in the face of such an energetic and dedicated priest.

»I don't even know how to explain this delay back in Cham. For an indefinite period, too. Abbot Berthold is really very angry. I couldn't have imagined that he would be so unwilling to talk.«

The honest man's dismay is audible, and I am so ashamed I wish I could sink into the ground. Now, my home parish has been dragged into this mess. What will the people in my hometown, who have placed their hopes in me, think? More expectations I cannot live up to. Has Father Greindl come to a final verdict on me? Perhaps there will be a chance, albeit late, to be understood.

»If I may, I would like to try to give you my view of things.«

»Please do. Maybe then things will become clearer.«

I tell him how I came to meditation and the heart prayer and what enormous importance they have in my life in connection with an intensive experience of God. Furthermore, how dialogue with like-minded people is especially important to me.

»You really must believe me,« I nearly implore.

Father Greindl's forehead wrinkles alarmingly, and the way he says nothing keeps me in suspense. What if he, too, fails to understand me? What will he report back home? And to my parents, who I have somehow been able to put off in my letters so far? Cold sweat is dampening my forehead.

He speaks after much deliberation.

»Your situation is complicated; I can see that. And I'm very, very sad that it's come to this. You can't expect the abbot to be accommodating at this time. On the contrary... He has refused any interference from me. I'm very sorry for you and for us.«

One small consolation is that he looks as devastated as I do. Maybe he can relate to what I am experiencing.

»At the very least, I have a gift for you. May it help you, especially in these difficult times.«

With these words, he hands me a record with songs by Dietrich Bonhoeffer.

Then he says an agitated goodbye, and I am alone again.

Almost... but for the music 'By gracious powers so wonderfully sheltered, and confidently waiting, come what may, So I would like to live these days together, and go with you into another year.

Yet is this heart by its old foe tormented, still, evil days bring burdens hard to bear; oh, give our frightened souls the sure salvation for which, O Lord, You taught us to prepare.

[...]

By gracious powers so wonderfully sheltered, and confidently waiting, come what may, we know that God is with us night and morning and never fails to greet us each new day.'

Is it thanks to these good powers and Father Greindl's intercession that a next meeting with Abbot Berthold is planned?

Only a few weeks later, nearly joyful news awaits me: next spring, I will be ordained a deacon! Finally, finally, finally! How long I have had to wait for this. Because that means …

»... but not that you should expect to be ordained a priest, Brother Christoph. However, we want to send you a clear signal: we won't let you fall, even if we may not follow you.«

I feel like I am falling from the clouds. It seemed that I was so close to my goal, towards which I have been working almost all my life – and then? Again, nothing. Again, I am left empty-handed. Deacon – what is that? A better assistant pastor. He does not hear confessions or celebrate Mass.

Of course not. That is the crux of the matter. It all makes sense now. I have still betrayed their trust. How naive of me to assume otherwise. As if I did not know how to separate my private and professional lives, could not distinguish confession from analysis, and did not understand the difference between absolution and psychotherapy. But a priest is responsible – and no one thinks I can be.

Once again, I have arrived exactly where I started in an abyss from which there seems to be no escape. Abbot Berthold truly knows no mercy.

On Saturday, the 26th of March, 1988, my mood is still in the pits. I hardly feel any pride about having reached this milestone. Will I even be allowed to achieve more?

As with the celebration of my solemn vows, my family is again sitting in the church. As best I can, I hide my feelings from them. When they ask questions, I make use of the truism ›good things take time.‹ It is not wrong. We are seeing each other today after a very long time. The auxiliary bishop from Regensburg celebrates the pontifical service for my deacon ordination. Perhaps it would have been a beautiful celebration if his sermon had not made me feel trapped.

»Because they are not of this world, they often encounter incomprehension, even scorn and mockery of their mission. The Lord knows that. And he knows that there is something else that is even more dangerous, namely the temptation to adapt to the world and thus to forget and finally abandon the very essence of their mission, namely the truth.«

What is this man talking about? Are his words a coincidence? Could it be? Does he not know the tug-of-war in the background that overshadows this celebration?

I can hardly concentrate on the ceremony. I cannot stop the dark thoughts running through my head. I feel as if the entire church world has conspired to denounce me, to judge me. Not only are my parents in the nave, but also a delegation from the Cham and Metten parishes. In the choir room, my monastic community, Father Greindl from Cham, as well as priests and monks from other monasteries, are apparently to hear how my lifestyle is being judged.

I feel so awful; I want to scream. Of course, I do nothing of the sort. I know what I am supposed to do. Only I cannot prevent myself from sobbing bitterly and having tears run down my face.

Since I have not succumbed to the temptation to conform but instead follow my truth, I must be content with the charitable offering of ordination as a Deacon. Does this decision by the head of the monastery and the senior council signify anything other than ›rejection?‹ Did not Abbot Berthold repeatedly express his ›lack of understanding‹ about my life's path several times? My efforts are met with ›scorn‹ and ›mockery,‹ as I well know.

I try to do only what I understand to be my ›mission:‹ to follow the path laid out within me in order to become better than I am. By following the hesychastic path with God's help and praying with the heart. Or by sitting in silence in order to fulfill my mission as a monk. To which the ongoing shadow analysis and critical dialogue with like-minded people also contribute. Behind this is not an end in itself, but God's work as I understand it: a very concrete plan that will lead me directly into HIS omnipresence, into divine unity. There can be no other way to become who I can be. That is what I have seen in my visions as a hermit. And it is true, »God knows that.«

Of course, HE knows that. He sees me, even in the dark of night. Even if I feel abandoned by the world, HIS protection is certain. HIS guidance, too.

Does this not mean that I am exactly where God thinks my place should be, here and now? Is it possible that HIS will is at work when this sermon so moves me? Should it give me a hint, make me think, and bring about a critical reflection so that I can contemplate my true nature? To make me aware of the new man who, because he is not of this world, does not make himself common to the human world?

In this light, I also have a different understanding of the person standing in a pillory. It does not emphasize my role as a victim, but in principle, underlines my prominent position in contrast to the followers in the crowd. Consequently, the sermon is not saying to me: »Keep it up, Brother Christoph!«

In fact, it proclaims the good news of my experience as a

hermit. Not yielding to the temptation to bend, to squeeze into a crack that is not made for me, just to escape the fall. Adaptation is narrowness, restriction, and limitation. It inevitably leads me into a downward spiral of further fears.

On the fifth night of my life as a hermit, what awaited me was already revealed: the freedom of boundless vastness. I find this vision confirmed in the wise address of the distinguished auxiliary bishop.

In an instant, my tears dry up. There is no reason to mourn. My whole being should rejoice: the promise of a new day has today been fulfilled.

Chapter 6: A New Day

As quickly as possible, I hurry to my meditation pillow, the graceful icon of the Virgin Mary firmly in view. She gives me reliable strength; I know that. Even now, when I am so agitated, almost out of breath, as if I had just completed a long-distance run and now need to catch my breath. Is that not exactly what has happened? How long was the distance I had to cover to get this far? It took years before I was allowed to be ordained. Years in which I was stuck as if in a swamp of rotting vines, losing myself more and more. Glimmers of hope remained scattered, never lastingly illuminating my inner night.

That is changing now. Everyone heard in the official sermon at my deacon ordination what I have to do: pursue my ›mission.‹ To trust in the new man within me, who is emerging from a process of decay over the recent years. Decay is transformation. The old dies. New comes. Dawn reliably follows the end of the night. And now?

Even in the light of a new day, Metten has not become a different place for me. What chances are there for me in this environment? Is there a place for me here? I doubt it. Behind these monastery walls, I will never be allowed to unfold or be truly myself. I have to broaden my horizon and think things differently. That is not possible in Metten over the long term.

That much is nearly certain.

The desperate effort to immediately find a valid answer to all my unanswered questions is only making me unhappy. Now my head is buzzing, and my euphoric mood seems to be slipping away. Annoyed, I close my diary. I do not even want to meditate. Instead, I just sit at my desk and let my somewhat cramped refuge have its effect on me. Small, but mine. And so nice and tidy. Everything is in the right place. Everything is so wonderfully organized. The necessary things are always within reach, ready at hand.

Only an arm's length away, for example, lies my worn-out copy of the ›Russian Pilgrim.‹ I leafed through it just this morning, then put it neatly back in its place next to the Bible.

I had hoped that reading it would give me a clue as to how things might develop for me. Some encouraging signs that my inner process of change had not faltered after all. Is there anyone willing to take on the honest responsibility of accompanying me in my new life as a deacon? That would make me feel more confident.

How I wish there was someone who would look after me, who knows who I am, who can understand what I have endured, someone who shares my perspective.

I am certainly able to count on Lejonidas, even if he is very busy. Attending his courses and the use of analytical therapy contributes enormously to my self-development. However…

Why have I never realized which name is on the cover? Only now, after staring seemingly without looking at it for minutes, has what I could have known a long time ago been made clear to me: The chance to be understood may be waiting for just a few kilometers away: The editor of the German edition of the Jesus Prayer lives in Niederalteich, a monastery not far from us. What an opportunity! Abbot Berthold had even pointed this out to me. That too only now comes to mind – where has my mind been these last months? When I mentioned the heart prayer during one of our crisis talks, he said that Father Gabriel lived not far from us.

How long ago was that conversation? I could have gotten in touch with the man long ago. Well, so what? »Don't get upset; just do it, Christoph!« I will myself to order.

I will try to make an appointment in Niederalteich as soon as possible. What a phenomenal end to a very eventful day.

Having learned from earlier experiences, I first ask Abbot Berthold for permission. Our fragile relationship does not need to be strained by further misunderstanding. Fortunately, he has no objection to the contrary. »Give him my warmest regards,« he calls out to me after he grants me his permission to visit the neighboring abbey. Why should he object? Father Gabriel is not only a monk but also an intellectual of great prestige, so he can only have a positive influence on me.

Now I want everything to happen very quickly; I have wasted too much time in the last months – years, actually. I urgently need a turnaround. Perhaps the secretary of the Ecumenical Institute noticed this when I called to ask for an appointment with Father Gabriel. At any rate, I am invited to come by very soon.

And suddenly everything is great, different, like new. After our first short conversation, I already have the feeling that I can breathe more easily. All sorts of oppressive things have suddenly fallen away. Even if not much at all has happened: I introduced myself, described the last stages of my monastic life, and reported in detail about my dissatisfaction, the feeling of stagnation, and lack of perspectives.

»If the prayer of the heart had not given me strength, fortified me, I would have been even more desperate these past months.«

In order to clear the thick lump in my throat, I quickly remember the positive news: »The ›Russian Pilgrim‹ has become a true friend of mine,« I call out with the genuine enthusiasm of an ardent devotee. »That's why I am so happy to finally get to meet you today. The book is so wonderful and strengthening! I think I just want to thank you for publishing such a treasure.«

I have not been this exuberant for a long time. There is something about Father Gabriel that invites me to speak freely. What an extraordinarily likable man! He is so different from the principled priests and brothers around me in Metten. There, no one seems to have the courage or the will to look beyond their own personal view, to look at new things, or to follow curiosity.

Encouraged and strengthened, I come out of this first meeting with a strong tailwind, so to speak. Maybe I just succeeded in preparing the ground for my new life. I feel deep gratitude that it has been so positive and that I have come so far.

Truly amazing how a lively dialogue developed within a very short time from this first meeting, I note in my diary, full of enthusiasm and self-satisfaction. Now not only do we see each other in his office, but I am also very welcome and well-received at the Niederalteich Monastery. Finally, I can spend my much-too-long days somewhere other than Metten.

What I especially appreciate is not having to pretend to be someone else anymore. Here I can just be: uncertain about the path to change, unsure, for example, about my career prospects. I am not expecting an offer to come from Metten. »I can't think of any job that would suit you. I'm sorry,« were Abbot Berthold's sober words, with which he marked another dead end for me, which makes it even more uplifting to be seen and recognized by such an important man as Father Gabriel. This is indeed a privilege.

I have the connection of the heart prayer, too, of course. Father Gabriel teaches it and has developed his own methodology, whereas Abbot Berthold knows it only in theory. That alone says enough about how heartfelt communion compares to my monastic community.

The neighboring abbey is… incomparable to my home monastery. The monastery's background says a lot for Niederalteich: Ecumenism! For me, this means greatness of mind, spiritual breadth, and the overcoming of boundaries. Here people think in a completely different way!

It is proving to be quite beneficial to me: »Could you imagine working here, at Niederalteich?«

I am dumbfounded and surely look a little foolish, with an open mouth and wide-open eyes.

»I see I've managed to surprise you. How nice!« Father Gabriel's lively laughter is contagious. I awaken from my state of shock and join in his laughter.

»Yeah, I didn't think there was a job opening here that I was fit for. I mean, one that's right for me.« What did I say? I am talking myself into a mess, but Father Gabriel is still smiling.

»Yes, I think you fit quite well with us. We have a staff shortage at the boarding school. We need teachers. I'll see what I can do for you.«

What? Kids! When I think back to my time with the altar boys, I would like to bail now. On the other hand, such an opportunity will not come again anytime soon. It is better than idly staring at the walls in Metten.

»I'm sure I've caught you off guard now. Just keep the idea in your head.«

»I like it!« I hear myself say.

»Are you sure? You still look surprised.«

»I am. But I think I'd like to try something new. I've spent so much time thinking and contemplating that I sometimes fear I've lost touch with the world, with my spontaneity and my instincts.«

Lost in thought, I pause for a moment. It takes a bit of preparation to be able to say the truth: »And I don't think it's good for me.«

»I appreciate your courage in venturing out in new directions,« he says with an appreciation that makes me feel self-conscious.

»I'm sure we will find a way for my abbot to contact yours to discuss the details. I'm sure Abbot Berthold won't mind ›lending‹ you to us.«

A firm handshake seals our agreement.

I am immensely proud; I only hope that no one finds a way to put obstacles in my path.

For the moment, my life is like a lucky streak: In September, I will become an educator. The two monastery leaders agreed to it and gave me a copy of their contract. With a salary and everything – even if it does go to Metten. My first real employment! And the best thing is: I will get to spend a lot of time in Niederalteich and will only occasionally return to my home monastery, maybe for a weekend. This arrangement comes pretty close to my idea of freedom.

If only it were not for the kids, even worse: rebellious teenagers between twelve and fifteen! Impudent answers, brazen disrespect, and suspicious youth magazines with articles on sex education. Not to mention the condom packs openly lying around, which make me reasonably confused, to say the least. It is impossible for me! Especially because nobody takes me seriously when I call for bedtime with an alarmingly shrill voice.

»Why? We're not doing anything!«

»I heard you talking just now.«

»Can't be because we haven't said a thing.«

»The voices came from this room, I'm sure of it.«

»Oh, you hear voices? You mean you're delusional? Oh,

this is serious! You should check in with my mother. She is a psychiatrist, and she'll make an appointment for you right away.«

Then the mocking laughter. It is almost more troubling to me than the impertinence of the much-maligned ›youth of today.‹ Without any experience in educating, I do not know how to react. This is not how I imagined my first job. What kind of impression do I give? Moreover, I do not want to overstretch the patience of my colleagues and all the brothers who believe in me. Now I have their support when they or even the director of the boarding school rushes in to put the notorious troublemakers in their places while I stand idly by, helpless. Things cannot go on like this.

Something must change. A glance at the regional telephone book tells me that an academy for educators is in Deggendorf, perfectly situated between Niederalteich and Metten. I make an appointment for a consultation as soon as possible, and it brings me the good news: not only can I start the ongoing training immediately, but I will also begin with the third year since I have already completed my theological studies.

Furthermore, I am easily able to combine my school day with my working hours at the boarding school. What a great coincidence! I am thrilled. In my mind, I already see myself describing my unruly students as a case study with my class as an audience. The brothers in Niederalteich also encourage me to start the training.

I also ask Abbot Berthold for his approval. Miraculously, he has no objections.

I spend less and less time in Metten these days. I am not drawn to my monastery. In Niederalteich, on the other hand, I am challenged and needed. During the week as an educator, and on the weekend, I gain my first experience as a deacon in church services. This would be unthinkable in Metten. But Niederalteich is also a special, bi-ritual monastery: here, services are celebrated not only according to the Roman Catholic tradition but also following Russian Orthodox liturgy, in which songs, gestures, images, and rituals express what happens at the bottom of the soul when it follows the path of Hesychia. The liturgy, in turn, shapes the souls being. What a wonderful interaction!

In this liturgy, the deacon has a special significance. The design of the church explains why: a white wall of icons, filled with representations of the Virgin Mary, evangelists, angels, and saints, divides the space of the faithful from the priest's sanctuary as a symbolic separation of heaven and earth. Behind it, the priests, singing with fervor, perform the sacred mysteries, invisible to the eyes of the faithful in the nave. In the Byzantine tradition, I have the honorable task of forming a connection between these worlds by wearing shining gold robes. Illustrious, I walk over the red marble to the iconic statues, singing ceremoniously, powerfully waving the incense burner. I bow reverently before all the golden shimmering witnesses of faith who had walked the path of God's love before me. From time to time, I can even preach and share my personal experience with the church. After the service, I happily take the opportunity to chat with the visitors. Quite often, very interesting conversations arise.

If only there were no Februaries. Every year the second month appears, bringing unpleasant conversations with it and bringing me back to another epoch. Will it be different this time? At the very least, I have made it somewhere in the meantime: I live a life according to the rules, under strict religious supervision, even if it is no longer permanently in my monastery. At the very least, it is with the abbot's explicit permission.

Who should find anything wrong with this picture? If something was, someone would have told me already. But I am worried: how stable is the foundation of my new self-confidence? Will it support me if Abbot Berthold puts pressure on me again? I do not know what to expect. Ultimately, my situation, which is based on an open alienation from my home monastery, is quite unusual. But since I have emerged from the daily tests of strength with my rebellious pupils as a future educator, I trust myself to engage in an open dialogue with the head of my monastery.

»There's not going to be another ordination for me, is there?«

I know the answer – yet I must ask. I want to clear the air.

Abbot Berthold sighs, shakes his head, resigned.

»Nothing has changed. You've become a stranger to us in recent years. We no longer understand you. These are not conditions for ordination.«

Although I expected nothing less, for a moment, my heart feels heavy. I pause briefly to think, breathe fully, and express what I had been thinking most deeply for a long time: »Father Abbot, it's already the third year that we are discussing whether or not I will be ordained a priest, and we seem to be getting nowhere.«

I summon up all my courage and say: »Could it be that behind the question of the coming ordination, there's another, completely different one, which is: Do we belong together or not?«

Abbot Berthold is silent. Only now do I realize how he has aged lately. Almost like he is bowed down in grief.

»Yes, Brother Christoph: I also feel that we have to make a new decision on this.«

»Right, I guess so. Maybe it was indeed the wrong decision in 1984 to make the permanent vows as a monk for life.«

How easily this simple truth slips my lips. I would have thought it harder for me to say the obvious: my struggle to find the right path has been in vain.

With a tired voice, Abbot Berthold begins again: »Like you, I gave careful thought in preparation for this conversation and discussed it with the Council of Seniors. The situation is hardly bearable for us as well. I have never experienced anything like this before, that such a procedure drags on for years.«

He sighs again.

He tenses his shoulders. »At the same time, this coming year will be an ›examination year‹ for you and for us.«

»An examination year? What's that?« Does that not just mean another year of uncertainty?

But Abbot Berthold does not look unfriendly. Things will go on for all of us; he seems to be telling me.

»Until February 1990, we, the monastic community in Metten and you on the other side will reconsider your vows.«

There must be a catch.

»Where am I supposed to think about this? In which monastery? Can I think about it at Niederalteich?« Just the idea of being imprisoned in Metten again is already weighing on me.

A small, very friendly smile flashes across Abbot Berthold's face.

»But of course. You may continue your work at the boarding school there and continue your education. You can decide for yourself where and how you want to spend your weekends, holidays, holy festivals, and public holidays; just let me know in advance.«

I am speechless as a terrific expanse spreads out in my mind. Is this what freedom looks like?

»Thank you for making this possible. I really appreciate the opportunity. Can I ask you one more question?«

»Of course.«

»Is there a precedent for this so-called ›examination year‹?«

The corners of his mouth curl up into a little smile. It makes him look a bit less haggard.

»Brother Christoph, what do you think?«

»A monk's vows are for life; there is nothing to test. Unless you just set a precedent, right?«

»Possibly.«

His look tells me everything I need to know. It has been a long time since I felt as deeply connected to my abbot as I do right now. I am almost sorry for the way I have thought of him in the times of my inner darkness when I could no longer distinguish who was on my side and who had turned against me. Simply by imposing this procedure, he surely did not only make friends. An abbot also has someone to report to.

It is still a long year until next February, and a lot can happen in that time. Unfortunately, no further conversation with Abbot Berthold, I note in my notes in May. Completely surprising the whole monastic community, he resigns a few months after our conversation for health reasons, we are told.

I am astonished. Abbot Berthold is not an old man. On the other hand... such a difficult office leaves its traces, of course. I had noticed a certain resignation and weariness in him. Difficult decisions sometimes take their toll, I think to myself.

Still, I am puzzled. In more ways than one. I also have to ask myself about the consequences of my bold ›examination year.‹ First of all, there is no longer anyone at all with whom I have to come to an agreement. Old abbot resigned, new one not yet elected. I have no point of contact, no one in Metten to overlook my actions. Another barrier has been broken, completely unforeseen. It was there a moment ago; now it is gone. How long have I wished for nothing more than to see such boundless freedom before me?

Yes, there is Father Prior. But he's nearly eighty years old and not at all as tough as Abbot Berthold. Besides, he is only the acting head of the monastery. He has more important things to do than deal with my case. Consequently, I am bound only to my conscience and my oath – which is currently undergoing critical examination, for the next several months.

And what if it is not? What if this trial period is now revoked? After all, it is without precedent in the church rules, so it could be ended under a new abbot just as suddenly as it was given to me. Is it not much more likely that the new abbot will insist on my oath's unbreakability? I have made a lifelong vow, after all.

A particularly dark night looms on the horizon again; the sunny views are already darkening. If I continue on this mental path, it will be as if the deeply felt satisfaction with the actual course of events had never existed. Then I will again be trapped in an equally endless universe of fear, self-doubt, and self-pity.

As always, when I do not know what to do, and I am beset by depressing thoughts, I first look at the image of my icon of Mary – as always, a reliable source of strength – before I immerse myself in the silence of meditation. Once again, I am not disappointed. Further pieces of the puzzle have come together and require reflection, I feel after I have emerged from the depth of contemplation. As so often before, it is my dream on the fourth night of my hermitage that once again demands my attention. It seems that there is still something missing in my interpretation.

Only now, in this constellation of inner and outer upheaval, does a detail catch my eye to which I gave too little importance when interpreting my dream: it was a female figure who showed me my true potential, who knew where I had to go. She helped me to understand that I must not hide if I want to experience expansion. Very interesting!

How strange that I neglected this aspect for so long. Yes, women do not play a big part in my life. But it need not stay that way.

As my examination year continues, I am again called upon to examine the options, to look at everything from a radically different angle. I already came a long way in this respect when I succeeded in reinterpreting supposed tragedy into meaningful inspiration. At a one-hundred-eighty-degree angle from my dismal outlook, a new day dawned – all I had to do was look at it properly. Exactly in the opposite direction from what I had previously thought.

I should do the same thing again now: think against my inner current. Why not consider women instead of men? The longer I think about it, the more attractive I find this alternative. Especially since I have not been able to give Lejonidas any satisfying feedback on how I am progressing with liberating myself from my attachments. Even if transforming sexual desire during meditation is still a great help, Homosexual lust remains preconsciously present. Does it have to be this way? Not necessarily. One hundred and eighty degrees away, a woman may know the way forward.

Might there be deeper meaning in the fact that I first think of Adelindis now? Of course, I can only ask my diary about such things since only it can keep secrets. I find it remarkable how often she attends our services lately. She is really nice to look at. I also met Barbara recently in the open contemplation group. She is a very sensible person, so spiritual and reserved.

Perhaps I should raise the subject with Prior Gabriel. But not just yet. It is better to wait for the next opportunity. At the moment, he's facing some extraordinary responsibilities because here, too, there is a change of leadership. 1989 is a hell of a year; the head of the monastery has also resigned in my second monastic home. The eighty-fourth abbot of Niederalteich will soon be succeeded by my new spiritual companion.

Finally, I get to have a private conversation with the remarkably dynamic and youthful new Abbot Albert of Metten during a walk through the monastery garden before I show him the boarding school premises. He has just completed his inaugural visit to his neighboring abbey and now spends time with me. Because he had previously been a pastor in a parish further away, we know each other only in passing.

No sooner have we said hello than I begin to tell him about myself. I talk about my continuing education, can report that it is already having a very positive influence on the rebellious boys, and I talk enthusiastically about my diaconate in Byzantine liturgy...

»... and I am also in the middle of a so-called examination year, although I have taken my vows, and I am now questioning my vocation. Maybe that's why I don't know where my place in the Metten community is. Besides, I consider myself homosexual.«

If Abbot Albert is surprised that I reveal these facts, he does not let it show. I get the impression he knows what is important in life. Confiding in him does not pose an incalculable risk. I know intuitively that this man will not judge me, which leads me to continue talking without interruption.

»Since I was young, I have been tormented by the conflict between my sexual inclination for men and my spirituality. But now it seems that therapy and meditation may have diminished my homosexual feelings – at the bottom of my being, I do not want to be a gay man,« breaks out of me at last. Never before have I so concretely expressed what I most wanted at the moment. I like the way the abbot listens to me; his concentrated silence encourages me to express what I really think. That alone is liberating.

»What matters is that you remain faithful to your solemn vows. This is important for two reasons: You are bound to celibacy, committed to a life without sex, and what does not happen makes little difference in terms of orientation. On the other hand, you still belong to the monastic community in Metten. We will see what the future brings us.«

That sounds just as friendly as Abbot Albert appears. He spoke with such serenity that the hint of chaos, which had seemed to be on the approach again, disappeared into nothingness.

In my euphoria over the surprisingly positive course of this encounter, it occurs to me only later that Abbot Albert did not say anything about the examination year explicitly. Right now, however, I am not interested in asking about it, but I assume that it has not suddenly been canceled just because the leadership in Metten has changed. So, it seems that I still have several months to make a major decision. It is time that I will need as well.

The question still stands like a monument in the room: ›Do we still belong together?‹ Do I still belong to Metten? Do I still see myself as a monk, even if, formally, I still am? If not, and I am certain that I am no longer the Armin who entered the monastery nine years ago, then I admit that former Abbot

Berthold question is right, who would I like to be? What kind of life do I want to lead? I will have to find the answer myself.

But at least I am not all alone. The recently elected Niederalteich Abbot Gabriel will accompany me in the process. The mere presence of the abbot often helps me, especially when I want not only to practice the heart prayer but to follow my free associations without trying to guess to which remote point of new self-knowledge they will lead me. He understands how to accompany me, maintains orientation, and does not lose sight of the goal. In every phase, he has his eyes on me. This takes away my fear of getting lost, of being stranded on the sidelines again. It is of great value to me to have him at my side when I formulate my self-chosen ›exam questions.‹ Sometimes with unsparing frankness: »What do you know about the connection between sexuality and spirituality?« Because the provocation of my own question makes me uneasy, I carry on talking in my usual manner until I feel that the person opposite has become familiar with my adventurous way of thinking.

»I ask because I wish to live a more tension-free life with my sexuality than I do now. Spirituality is a basic element of my life. That also seems to be true with my sexuality. Thanks to intensive contemplation, it runs in energetically-ordered paths and does not endanger my celibacy. I am simply interested – purely hypothetically, of course – in what happens at its intersection. What could happen.«

Abbot Gabriel remains remarkably calm.

»I see.«

That is all I can get out of him so far. But surprise would sound different. That is a good sign. I feel encouraged to continue.

»The idea of wanting to think these two things together is not new either. It's been on my mind for quite some time. Last year, when I tried living as a hermit for a week, I received a sign that I should continue thinking in this direction. My path leads *only* in this direction, the message said.«

His attentive look and silence invite me to go one step further.

»Therefore, in this phase in which I am urgently called upon to review my life planning, the question naturally arises for me as to where this synthesis can be found. I believe that my destiny will only be fulfilled where they meet.«

Like on hot coals, I await his answer. I did not expect his mischievous smile.

»What makes you think I know the answer?«

»I trust in your knowledge,« I simply say.

»Then, of course, I must not disappoint your trust.«

With an old-fashioned key, he opens an inlaid bookcase that I have often admired. I have never been allowed to look at a book from it. Today I find out why: »Here I keep that literature which is better kept hidden. The contents of my poison cabinet are usually secret.«

He selects a large book and puts it on the oak table in front of me. The cover shows two figures richly decorated with gold, who could have come from the Byzantine liturgy. If it were not for their positions: straight as a candle, closely entwined. Even if a first association makes me think of the mandala picture of Niklaus von der Flüe, the erotic character of the cover is undeniable. The title speaks volumes: ›The Great Book of Tantra. Sexual Secrets and the Alchemy of Ecstasy‹. My hand is already approaching the book – I really want to flip through the pages – when it disappears again. The big key turns in the lock, and the treasure is shut away.

A wave of disappointment surges up and dies away again. I came so close to understanding more, to penetrating even deeper mysteries. At least I have been given a hint in which direction I should think. My voice of reason knows that I cannot ask for more.

Then the abbot says: »Now you know that tantric philosophy postulates a connection between sexuality and spirituality. That's all I can tell you.«

I have genuine respect for his frank words, which are, of course, contrary to Catholic doctrine. He has gone very far to accompany my self-development. That is not to be taken for granted.

However brief the sight of the book may have been, its effect did not miss its mark. My ears glow, my body is on fire as I hurriedly retire to my monastery cell. I must meditate immediately to find my center again in silence, to calm my mind.

Sometime later, my body is back in balance, but my mind circles faster than expected around the sole question of where I can get this book.

I long for my evening meditation group. The surroundings will do me good. There I will also see Barbara again. Her sensible manner will be a wonderful counterbalance to my restlessness.

»You're so different today.«

Adelindis. As usual, she speaks her mind. »Different? Different how?« I try to play down her intuition. It is too public here.

»There's such tension around you. You're literally on fire,« says Adelindis with a radiance that makes me a little confused.

»It must be my headache. Probably the cool evening air will help best,« I hear myself say, inexplicably giddy. Adelindis reads it as a message.

»Yeah, I was just leaving too.«

Although I was not able to get closer to Barbara as I had hoped – apart from a cursory greeting, I did not speak a word to her today – I suddenly find myself alone with Adelindis in the twilight.

»What's the matter?«

Her way of getting straight to the point irritates me.

»Tantra.« I cannot help but answer with a single word.

»Tantra?« She is happy. » Oh, how nice!«

»Hm. I saw a book today that I can't get off my mind.«

Adelindis' happy laughter echoes through the street. Unpleasantly surprised, I look around. »Not so loud. What will people think?«

She refuses to give in.

»If you're interested in Tantra, then I know something for you.« Her hair shines in the light from the streetlamp.

»Oh, yes. A book?« I ask eagerly. This is exactly what I was looking for. Some literature that will not be taken out of my hands.

»Better than a book. ›Home games.‹«

I feel a rare fascination. I don't really care what she's talking about.

»I don't know what home games are. What is it?«

Her blue eyes sparkle, an insane promise comes from her.

»I can't explain that. It's about doing things, practical work.«

Then she is laughing again. I am stunned.

»Are you free Friday night?«

I nod, fatigued.

»Is 8:30 okay?«

I nod.

»I'll give you my address.«

Not on a piece of paper. She scribbles the street and the number in the palm of my hand. Oh, what the...?

»See you. Bye.«

And she's gone. She turns around again and winks.

It can happen that fast. Suddenly, I have a date, the first date of my life. And also an appointment to learn the practice of Tantra. Up close and personal. What else could she have meant?

An exam year is a great thing: I am free to do anything, to try out anything that might help me to find myself.

On Friday after the Compline, the Night Prayer, I sneak on tiptoe out of the monastery's garden gate. Under cover of darkness and my night-black habit, I hope to reach Adelindis' house, which lies on a small hill in the village, unseen. I ring the doorbell, enormously tense inside. Nobody opens.

What am I doing here? If someone from the neighborhood were to see me now, even recognize me. A parishioner, perhaps. There, next door, the curtain moved. Someone is watching me, sees how I – a monk! – make a house call to a young woman at night. Terrible, terrible, terrible. I should leave. Right away.

The moment I am about to disappear again into the darkness, the door opens, and Adelindis grabs my hand without hesitation and pulls me into the small corridor. To close the front door behind me, she presses herself against me. She is not wearing much, and I can feel very clearly the curves of her body.

The countless candles that bathe the entire ground floor in festive light makes me even warmer. My senses are already confused, and I hardly know what I am doing.

Next thing I know, I find myself sitting on an ottoman by candlelight. Adelindis is right by my side. From cocktail glasses, we drink a red liquid that tastes like nothing I know.

»Martini Rosso. The perfect complement to ›house games.‹«

Adelindis is so close to me that I hear her voice right next to my thoughts. Her sensuous perfume, the stimulating martini, and this magic word pull me even further under her spell. I have no idea what it means. But she will show me. Soon. Our evening has just begun.

»I'm taking part in a one-year tantra training course. Margot Anand, the director, regularly gives us ›house games.‹ Which means nothing less than practice, practice, practice perfecting what we learn from her. You understand?«

»Hmmm.«

While her voice continues to bewitch me, she draws imaginary lines on my chest with her index finger. The many layers of habit do not impede the comforting electrification of my body. I close my eyes and surrender myself completely to the stream of my feelings. I feel free from any pressure, free down to the tips of my toes, which is probably due to the fact that she has taken off my shoes and socks, as I realize after a very long time in surprise.

When? How? I do not know. Have I not felt her touch on my chest the whole time?

»Come.«

I willingly follow her.

On our way to her bedroom, I lose more clothes. I enter the room, having left my habit behind me. I am greeted by a true sensual intoxication: a splashing indoor fountain, an intense scent of incense, sparkling harp music, and colorful autumn flowers everywhere.

As if she cast a spell over me, I let myself be seduced as if in slow motion to a refined sequence of ritual touches that open the mind to the extended union of Shiva and Shakti. Breathtaking! I cannot recall any single point of culmination because it does not exist.

Much occurs on an energetic level that is familiar to me. How many times have I had to secretly transform my sexual desires? Today it is the center of the magical power of Tantra, to which Adelindis initiates me. And what an initiation experience it is. For me, it is only comparable with divine enlightenment.

At dawn, I again transform myself into a modest monk and secretly walk back to the monastery on winding paths. I manage to attend Matutin and Laudes on time and thereby join the other monks in the night and morning prayers.

This time I have no sense of guilt. I am not afraid to look my confreres in the eye. I join the choir singing with my head held high. My spirit is free; my whole being feels purified. I have arrived at a whole new level.

That was completely different after being with Amatus. Back then, it was nearly impossible for me to bear the burden of my guilt. And my fear of losing control was immense when I was with him.

None of that is happening now. This time, I could just give in and let go. This probably has to do with the fact that I have successfully alienated myself from homosexual lust. This shadow no longer dominates my existence – otherwise, I would not have been able to enjoy the tantric ritual with Adelindis so much, completely absorbed in being. Deep, meditative, and real: that is how the night felt. Above all, it is unbelievable for me to use these words in a sexual context – so far, I have only known them in my religious practice. I would describe my experience of God like this. And now this.

Most importantly, the validity of the visions from my week of retreat has once again been confirmed. The two will no longer be separable in my life. Two sides, one coin: no more sexuality without spirituality. I have known since the fourth day that I cannot live any other way. Now, to have been initiated into this dimension, to be seized and lifted up by this tantric energy, is, of course, different from the abstract ideas in my notes.

Where do things go from here?

Day four and five of my visions have arrived. Now I must boldly think forward and expect my brothers to realize that I am no longer one of them and for them to want me to go on my own way. My spiritual fire wishes to blaze, not disappear as a tiny flame under a bushel of monastic conventions.

February is not far off when another final decision is expected from me. My training will also be finished next year. I might be able to gain a foothold in secular life as an educator. There are some things to consider, however. My examination year is not yet over.

When the time comes, I know the news that I must deliver to Abbot Albert. To the question whether my attitude toward Metten has changed in 1990, I can answer unambiguously: »No. Not in the least. Not much connects me with my home monastery anymore. And I do not feel a new love for monastery and community, not from either side.«

»Would you consider a transfer to Niederalteich? You feel very well there; you seem to meet with much goodwill in that community.«

Oh, this is a surprise. So is his worried tone of voice. The conversations from the past few years were quite different.

A transfer to Niederalteich. It would not be completely out of the question. Was not, anyway, at an earlier time. But it is also a monastery, so I know it is not the right place for me. I need to go somewhere else. I need something else entirely. I am sure of it. The monastery has nothing more to teach me. I have experienced God with all my senses. Now it is time to take a different path, taking my new experiences with me.

I shall tell Abbot Albert nothing less. This way, there can

only be one decision for me: »Perhaps I am even called to a life of marriage and family. I want to find that out as much as I want to link my experience of God with sexuality.«

Contrary to my expectations, Abbot Albert nods understandably. Did he see my new life coming?

»It is good that your crisis of purpose has finally come to an end, and you have found inner clarity again. Of course, I would have wished you a future in our monastery. But, of course, I respect your decision. You have not made it easy for yourself to make this decision; all your brothers know that.«

In Abbot Albert's words, the odyssey of my recent past sounds rather rational and objective. Quite different from what I experienced. At least those dramas are behind me now.

»Then let us agree on August 1, 1990, as your resignation date; until then, you can still save some money. I will have a bank account set up for you, to which your salary, which goes to our monastery, will be transferred from now on so that you will have your own funds at your disposal to facilitate your new start.«

I am stunned. My thoughts had not looked so far ahead. How foresighted Abbot Albert is.

»In the coming weeks, I will send all the necessary documents concerning your withdrawal from the Order and your discharge from deacon ordination to the Roman Curia. If they approve, your monastic life will be concluded.«

Yet, my life has not come to an end but is only just beginning. Completely new. I will create a whole new life for myself and reinvent myself completely.

I already know who I want to have by my side in this new life. I am glad that she feels the same way and can imagine a life with me. It is especially important to me to know that Barbara is deeply rooted in her faith. She takes heart prayer seriously, like me, and has conservative values. Quite different from the extroverted and brash Adelindis. Barbara is the right, down-to-earth woman for me.

In spring, the elderly prior of the Metten monastery dies, not entirely unexpected. As chance would have it, the funeral takes place on the same day that I have an appointment with Abbot Gabriel for one of our special talks.

My decision to leave the monastic world and to undertake a secular new beginning is, for him, not controversial but consistent. He has actively accompanied my struggle to find the right path over the past months.

One thing is certain anyway: Niederalteich will always remain a very special place for me. I have always found my own personal story in the monastery's more recent history; the reunification of the separated, the spirit of unity. How many strands came together for me at Niederalteich? If ecumenism is unity – does that also mean internally?

This is what I have been after for so long. Here I was heard. And perceived. And encouraged, even emboldened to follow my path. A path that need not necessarily lead to isolation. I did not live here in the monastic community as an eccentric outsider on edge, because there was a place for me in its middle. In a monastery that has been given the task of furthering this very unity.

This mission originates from an abbot in the 1950s who, since his novitiate, was so touched by Jesus' call to his disciples, which the abbot understood as an appeal that he believed can be read in the high priestly prayer: *I pray that they may all be one. Father! May they be in us, just as you are in me and I am in you. May they be one so that the world will believe that you sent me.*

I gave them the same glory you gave me, so that they may be one, just as you and I are one: I in them and you in me, so that they may be completely one, in order that the world may know that you sent me and that you love them as you love me... (Gospel of John, Chapter 17, Verse 21-23). Only together, not as individuals, will they be able to powerfully proclaim the Lord's message.

Because this abbot literally interpreted a directive of Pope Pius XI, who, as a reaction to the revolutionary upheavals in Russia, wanted to integrate Russian Orthodox theology and liturgy into Roman Catholic congregations, Niederalteich became my spiritual home.

Decades later, the Second Vatican Council not only underlined the need to overcome Christian division in favor of the unity of all people but also called for cooperation with other religions in order to renew Christianity. This led Father Anton to the Far East, from where he returned as a Zen master who taught me silent meditation in Würzburg. Knowing this immersion method has helped me to soothe my emotional pain and to transform sexual pleasure into pulsating energy streams within my body. Without this knowledge, I would not have had any idea how to live in celibacy.

Finally, I am also indebted to Abbot Berthold: If he had not sent me and the others to Würzburg, I would not have met Lejonidas in the house of St. Benedict. Would I then have ever learned about Christian contemplation and about the prayer of the heart? In the end, this led me to Niederalteich, into the custody of Father Gabriel, who contributed like no other to my inner liberation. Today feels like a homecoming because I have finally found what I have been searching for all along.

How many wishes have come true for me in this monastery?

As always, Gabriel sums it up: »Just as the periphery of the circle returns to itself and closes again, so in this reversal the spirit returns to itself and becomes one.«

Had I not been able to gather and unite my strength in the heart prayer, I probably never would have made it this far. On that, I completely agree with him.

As always, I offer my hand to Gabriel in parting. Today, however, something strange happens. He does not shake it but holds it and asks me to kneel down. Not knowing what he is doing, I do what he asks.

He puts both hands on my head and says a quiet prayer, blessing me.

Alas, time is short; I must hurry to reach the cemetery on time. I have no time to think about what has just happened. I quickly say goodbye and hurry to the car. However, this touching gesture refuses to let me go, in the truest sense, distracting me even during the funeral service.

As I stand with my brothers at the open grave, the coffin lowered into the opening in the earth, and each of us adds a handful of dirt, I suddenly understand the moment of farewell in Gabriel's blessing: he has released me from his spiritual guidance. I am no longer his spiritual disciple but his equal friend and companion. Evidently, he trusts me to pursue my inner and outer path of transformation without his constant guidance. I would never have expected this when I first sought to talk to him last year in my truly disheveled state.

Call, profession, and vocation have now been revealed

under his guidance, and I know I am on the best path to inner healing. Everything will be healed. Because unity wants to be lived.

In principle, life as a monk ends only with his death. A resignation during one's lifetime is not part of any set of rules and regulations, so it should not occur and, therefore, cannot be officially celebrated.

But that now completely contradicts how I feel. I am grateful for the past years. I do not want my time in the monastery to be treated as a bureaucratic act that is ended by formalities, even if it is the bureaucratic apparatus of the Vatican that brings it to an end.

I want festivity, ceremonies in which I, in my church ministry, which I will only hold for a short time longer, take center stage.

Why should I not? I am free to do what I want now. So, if I want to celebrate my departure with all the monks, then so be it. Even if I must create all the rituals, I want myself.

I begin with the Easter Vigil in Metten: confident, I step into the semicircle of the sacristy as a deacon. At the beginning of the celebration, I look at the abbot and my fellow brothers: »I enjoy being a deacon very much. But today, I celebrate my last Eucharist in this ministry with you.« Abbot Albert concludes the greeting »Procedamus in pace…«

to which all the priests and monks unanimously answer, »…in nomine Jesu Christi, amen,« and cross themselves. »Let us go in peace, in the name of Jesus Christ, amen.«

Carried by this dignified celebration, I look forward to the Byzantine Easter liturgy at midnight. In Niederalteich, I am warmly welcomed and embraced by my brothers there. Like me, they are looking forward to the forthcoming service. With solemn high spirits, I serve for the last time as a mediator between the faithful and the holy priesthood in the monastery church. I feel HIS presence today even more intensely than usual, allowing no melancholy to arise, only quiet joy over HIS everlasting guidance. That I can always be sure of.

And I need that more than ever when I receive a call in Niederalteich from my father. When my father himself reaches for the phone, it must be serious. I am on alert. Although my life has taken another unexpectedly sharp turn, my relationship with my parents is surprisingly stable. The physical distance of the monastic years has done us good. My father even managed to sound respectful when he heard about my imminent departure from the monastery. He told my mother that he was not really surprised; I always had a mind of my own.

My mother then wrote further: *He is more concerned with the question of renouncing his inheritance. He wants to undo it. Soon you will no longer be a monk, and you will be able to take up your inheritance again.*

I could not have cared less. But for me, inner unity also includes a harmonious relationship with my parents. Both parents. Although my mother is still a little closer to me and our communication is stronger.

So, it is even more worrying when she is not the one to contact me but my father. »Hospital... thrombosis... critical condition.«

I do not need to hear anymore before I hurriedly make my way to the hospital in Cham. She looks pale and weakened, hardly reminiscent of the vital soon-to-be mid-fifty-year-old who I last saw at my deacon ordination.

»My time is running out.«

A cold hand seems to reach for my heart. I must breathe in and out deeply. Although she looks so bad, can only speak with difficulty, I had been clinging to the hope of her speedy recovery. With God's help.

»And I'm ready to go. Will you administer the Anointing of the Sick tomorrow?«

»Of course!« I answer impulsively. When in her last hours on earth she sees in me the ecclesiastical dignitary, I must naturally fill this role. I am fully aware of this special responsibility.

The next day I first go to Metten. From the sacristy, I fetch the Officiale, from which I must read the course of the rite. With book and balm, I visit my mother once again at her hospital bed.

As I place the purple stole over my habit; I pray that by doing so, I will be able to grant her last wish: to be held by Jesus Christ, secure in the Catholic faith so that she can depart in peace. It is only on my journey home that I realize what I have overlooked in the midst of the rush of events: actually, I should have refused her this last request – as a deacon, I am not authorized to administer this sacrament. A deep sigh rises from my breast. Have I deceived her in her last hours?

After I reflect deeply on it, I prefer to answer in the negative. Does the validity of the sacrament play a role in retrospect? Most importantly, I was able to give my mother some comfort in the face of her death. That is all that really matters.

She passes away four days later.

On May 2, we gather for her funeral service in the parish church of St. Jacob, my home parish. There they had once waited for the celebration of my First Mass. Now I return home as a grieving son.

The young assistant pastor holds the service, with Abbot Albert from Metten at his side and several other priests who are acquainted with my family. The fact that my abbot is among the concelebrants at the altar of the Holy Mass and that I am seated in a simple black suit in the front pew next to my family emphasizes in front of everyone how my monastic community and I stand to each other: we are reconciled but remain deeply united. All adversities have been overcome.

Apart from the pain of my mother's premature death, the coincidence of the events moves me deeply: it was only her death that led me to take my seat on this pew as a parishioner, among many others – without the office of a church. Thick tears run unrestrained down my cheeks. The significance of her death, which from this perspective has contributed to my reconciliation with the official church, touches me to the core.

Br. Christoph-Armin Heining OSB

Mauritiushof 3

8351 Niederaltaich

May 24, 1990

Holy Congregations

For the Doctrine of Faith

and for The Institutes of Consecrated Life

and the Communities of Apostolic Life

congregatio pro Doctrina Fidei

et congregatio pro Institutis vitae apostolicae

et Societatibus vitae apostolicae

Request for Dispensation from the Diaconate, return to the lay state and dismissal from the Order.

Excellency, Most Reverend Cardinal,

In the thirtieth year of my life, the ninth year of my profession, and at the beginning of the third year of my diaconate, I ask you, Excellency, after careful consideration, for my return to the lay state and for my dismissal from the order. The realization that, for me, the form of life of marriage and family is the more appropriate leads me to approach you with this request.

I, Br. Christoph-Armin Heining, was born on August 9, 1960, in Cham/Bavaria. After completing my school education with the Abitur, I entered the Benedictine Abbey of Metten/Lower Bavaria.

At the end of the novitiate, I made the temporary profession on October 30, 1981, and the solemn profession on October 24, 1984. My ordination to the diaconate and priesthood was originally planned for 1986/87, i.e., after completing my theological studies at the Catholic

Theological Faculty of the University of Würzburg (1981-1986) with the diploma and the pastoral year (1987). In the school year 1987/88, I worked as a religion teacher and catechist in the monastery parish of Metten. During this time, I was ordained a deacon on March 26, 1988.

In the fall of 1988, I was released to work in the boarding school of the neighboring Abbey of Niederaltaich. I am now completing my second year of teaching at the school.

Since my 1st Profession, I have spent most of my time outside Metten Abbey. During my theology studies, I began to study intensively the spiritual tradition of the Eastern Church, including its forms of meditation and prayer. I made my solemn profession in devotion and enthusiasm for Christ, but in my lack of maturity, I overlooked the concrete situation of the Metten monastery and the far-reaching consequences of the vows.

Already in 1986, this inner development of mine had led to a strong dissent, as a result of which the Abbot did not permit me to be ordained a deacon as originally planned. Also, in 1987 the Abbot rejected my request for ordination – in consultation with the Senior Council. After my return from the pastoral year in 1988, I again applied for admission to the diaconate, convinced that this was my vocation, my form of life with Christ. The Abbot and Senior Council had concerns, but they approved the ordination as deacon to give me a sign of belonging to the Abbey; they did not want to let me fall. The admission to the priestly ordination in the same year, however, was firmly refused. They were afraid that, as a priest, I would not be able to live up to their ideas and those of the Abbey and of the church, especially with regard to the administration of the Sacrament of Confession.

My work as an educator in the Niederaltaich boarding school from the fall of 1988 was a good solution for the Metten monastic community, for me, and for the Benedictine monastery of Niederaltaich for the further common path of life. The connection to Metten Abbey, however, loosened more and more so that in the spring of 1989, at a meeting with the Abbot, it was clear to everyone involved that ordination to the priesthood was out of the question at that time. It also became clear to us that a fundamental reassessment of my monastic vocation was necessary. Therefore, by Easter 1990, a new decision should have been made in this regard.

At my request, the Abbot and the Senior Council, therefore, also made the time that remained free from my work in the boarding school available to me on my own responsibility for a more comprehensive examination.

During this past year, through my work with the students in the boarding school, I have become aware that my love for Christ wants to be realized in love for neighbors. The failure of my desired vocation, that of a religious priest has opened my eyes to the fact that this love for the neighbor wants to find expression in my life in the form of marriage and a family.

Your Excellency, Most Reverend Cardinal, I am grateful that I was able to live for ten years in the religious community of the Benedictines in Metten and that during these years, I was able to find my way closer to Christ. I feel very connected to the Catholic Church and will be grateful to be able to live and work in harmony with the church as a layperson in my further life.

Br. Christoph-Armin Heining

Letter to the Communities of Apostolic Life Congregation:

My time as a monk comes to its conclusion at the end of July 1990. On my last day in Metten, I realize without surprise that although I love the community, there is really nothing to keep me here. Never have I been so aware of how much the unchanging routines tell me that time has stopped. Nothing changes; nothing moves forward. What promised stability when I entered the monastery paralyses me today and stops me in my flow.

My suitcase has long since been packed, my cell cleared out, and I am ready to give my cowl and robes back to the tailor. But first, I am supposed to attend lunch – with all the procedure around it: first the noon choir, then the procession – with hood on – into the dining hall.

A twenty-five-minute lunch with soup and a dessert accompanied by a table reading. Afterwards, the procession – with hood on – back to the choir. Then, the short prayer of the abbot in conclusion.

In the afternoon, the time to say goodbye has finally come. The brothers are celebrating Father Uwe's name day with a coffee break. One last time I sit at the table with them – now in suit pants and a shirt. A very unusual feeling after many years in a monastic uniform. After coffee and cake, I say goodbye to everyone present with a strong handshake. And with an expression of gratitude for the very instructive and deeply formative years I spent here.

Still, I look forward to spending the very last days of my monastic life in Niederalteich, where I have enjoyed living the past months with all my heart.

Prot. 79/90/D

Beatissime Pater,

CHRISTOPH-ARMIN HEINING, O.S.B.

diaconus a votis perpetuis professus in ORDINE S. BENEDICTI

ad pedes S.V. provolutus, humiliter postulat dispensationem ab
oneribus in sacro Diaconatus ordine susceptis et indultum
discedendi a praefato Ordine S. Benedicti (O.S.B.)
ob rationes in relatione allatas.

* * * * *

Die 6 Octobris 1990
Congregatio de Cultu Divino et Disciplina Sacramentorum, vigore
specialium facultatum sibi a SS.mo Domino Nostro IOANNE PAULO
PAPA II   tributarum, attentis peculiaribus circumstantiis
in casu concurrentibus et   commendatione Supremi Moderatoris
Ordinis S. Benedicti
Eidem benigne committit ut, pro sua prudenti discretione, valeat
dispensare oratorem ab oneribus diaconatus et concedere indultum
discedendi ab eodem Ordine S. Benedicti

Paterne   eum   hortabitur   ut   ad   sacramenta
Paenitentiae et Eucharistiae frequenter accedat ac per bonos
mores et opera christianae pietatis aliis exemplo praeluceat.

Servetur insuper, pro posse, Can. 702,2.
Contrariis quibuslibet non obstantibus.

(E. Card. Martínez, Praefectus)

(R. Melli, Subsecretarius)

CONGREGATIO DE CULTU DIVINO

ET DISCIPLINA SACRAMENTORUM

Prot. 79/90/D

Holy Father,

Christoph-Armin Heining, O.S.B.

A Deacon and a member who is perpetually professed in the Order of St. Benedict

kneeling at the feet of your holiness, in humility requests a dispensation from the burdens and demands he has received in the order of deacon and an indult of departure from the aforementioned Order of St. Benedict (O.S.B.) **for the reasons cited in the report.**

* * * * *

on 6 October 1990

The Congregation for Divine Worship and the Sacraments, by the power of the special faculties given to the tribunal by our SS.mo Pope John Paul II, **taking into account the particular circumstances in the case and with the recommendations of the Superior of the** Order of St. Benedict: -
Therefore, the Congregation, according to its own prudent discernment, hereby grants a dispensation from the burdens of the diaconate and an indult of departure from the burdens of this same order of S;Benedict.

Paternally encourage him to approach the sacraments Reconciliation and the Eucharist frequently as a model for other works of piety and good manners.

Be safeguarded, and, moreover, as much as possible, with Can. 702.2. Things to the contrary all things to the contrary notwithstanding.

E. Card. Martinez Praefettus)

(R Melli, undersecretary)

Chapter 7: Being One

Have not all my wishes come true, just as I had foreseen during my week living as a hermit? I feel truly content and happy. Saying goodbye to my brothers in Metten and to the monastic community in Niederalteich not only went smoothly but it was also celebrated with appropriate festivity and dignity. Now the next phase of life is ready to begin.

Leaving my bare monastery cell behind, I call a pretty room under the cozy pitched roof of a Franconian half-timbered house my new home starting August second. It is my first apartment, all to myself, and I feel a bit proud of my small empire. It is also conveniently located in the middle of Fürth, Germany, making it just a short distance from my workplace in Nuremberg.

How I got it is a story all its own. Even if my father calls it ›pure coincidence‹ I see the divine plan behind all the fateful turns of events that led me to a job at the Caritas Pirckheimer House in Nuremberg. While I was still at the monastery, I saw myself working there in a memorable dream. What else could it mean but that I should apply there for a job? Needless to say, the next day, I had nothing more important to do than look up the number of the Diocesan Adult Academy from the telephone book and make a call, my heart beating. Again, I was lucky! They were looking for a pastoral officer for the youth education department, and the position needed to be filled by September 1st.

They mean me! I rejoiced inwardly.

After an encouraging telephone call with the director of the house, Jesuit Father Claus Huber, I enthusiastically send my application to the Archdiocese of Bamberg, who were financing the position. I expected a quick answer. September was approaching, and I considered myself qualified, although I knew little about the tasks of a pastoral officer.

Disappointingly, I receive no answer. Still, I was not ready to give up. I had envisioned myself working in the Caritas Pirckheimer House, and so it must be. My trust in the deeper meaning of the dream was unbroken. Maybe I just had to help a little. In no circumstances was I going to put up with nothing, with silence. So, I called Father Huber again. I felt that we were on the same wavelength the first time I talked to him. Maybe he could put in a good word for me?

It took several tries before I finally got him on the phone – with mixed news: »Unfortunately, your pastoral year and your two years working as an educator with academic training do not qualify you to be a pastoral officer,« I heard him say.

Before I could feel any sense of disappointment, he continued: »But I have already inquired in Bamberg as to whether the archdiocese could not adapt the job description to your qualifications. Please be patient. It will still take some time.«

Not to worry, I was quite happy to summon the patience that could bring me closer to my goal. And for it, I am rewarded. The good news reaches me a short time later by mail: On September 1, 1990, I may start a part-time job as a pastoral assistant in the second training year.

Guided and uplifted, I feel safe and secure in the way things seem to be naturally unfolding. My new life is indeed beautiful.

That is, it could be nice if it were not for Barbara by my side. She is with me quite often because the journey between Erlangen and Fürth is not far, and we are trying to get to know each other. At least, that was the plan when I left the monastery: attempting a normal relationship with a woman. It just does not seem to be working out as I thought.

I am overwhelmed by the temptation to pay more attention to attractive men than to her. Naturally, this does not escape her attention and results in heated scenes.

»You're always looking at some guy. You know what I don't get? Why are we even together?«

»Not so loud! What will people think?«

I look around in horror. Did anyone hear us? It was loud enough. I feel embarrassed.

»Oh, so you're interested in what complete strangers think?«

She snorts angrily, shaking her head.

»But how I feel, your so-called girlfriend, you don't care about. You have no feelings for me. Why should you? I'm not a man!«

Alarmed by her words, I try to make myself heard.

»Are you finished? Can I say something?«

My attempt does not go over well.

»Am I finished? You're asking me if I'm finished? Are you serious?«

She looks at me as if she's about to jump down my throat.

»That's right. I'm done. With you. I've been done with you for a long time. So goodbye«

What does she mean, goodbye?

»Barbara? Barbara! Come back!«

There is nothing to be done. She is gone and does not turn around again. She just left me. I was not expecting that. She used to be so understanding. I do not know what has gotten into her.

I momentarily squint my eyes, overwhelmed by the shame of having been dumped on the promenade. Then I take a deep breath and ask myself what I am going to do now. First, meditate. In my new home, I have already found three places that are run by Father Anton's students. If I am lucky, at least one is open now. I urgently need a conflict-free space and to reconnect with the meditation community. My life as a monk out in the world might not be as problem-free as I had imagined.

On the way to the nearest meditation center, I reflect, asking myself the question: How did it come to this? Did I not start my new life with the best intentions and resolutions? My relationship with Barbara seemed to fit so perfectly with my idea of a normal life, the kind led by other men everywhere.

If only conflicting emotions were not always getting in the way of my plans. I cannot get rid of the magnetic attraction I feel for handsome men. I look at them involuntarily, unable to glance away.

Have I not already progressed much further than this? Did not my life after the night with Adelindis already shine in a new, wonderful light? It had literally shown that a relationship with a woman was possible, did it not? Is the model I envisioned for my life already a failure?

I feel much better after an extended meditation session in the company of my community. My orientation is back; my inner compass has settled down again as if I am resting within myself. I think this has something to do with living in a shell.

This is exactly what was recently revealed to me in an impressive vision: A pastel-colored housing with a circular opening at the base, tapering upwards like a tower. This delicate structure constantly rotates around its own axis, so the spiral structure is constantly in motion. What I see is something like a spiral staircase that winds its way up carefully but continuously. Does it depict my path of inner transformation? Indeed, it does not run in a straight line, and yet I move forwards. At my individual pace and not always as fast as I would like to. Yet I advance towards the Tabor lamp, the highest divine light.

The longer I reflect on the image of this spiral-shaped tower of the ›common tower shell‹, the more I like it. Retreating into meditation, as now after the situation with Barbara, is like retreating inside my inner house. It is both a protective space and a source of strength for me. I once spent a week in such seclusion to escape the lack of perspective within my monastery cell. Only as a hermit, detached from the world, in complete seclusion, did I feel hope for a completely new way of opening my mind right into the heavenly dimension that Lejonidas spoke of so often.

In fact, I came out of that week with some very important insights: looking at the lives of those around me, envious of their accomplishments, only made me unhappy. I do not lead their lives, only my own. My life proceeds on a path in which I repeatedly meet men who interest me. There is no use denying that if I want to stay honest. This was made clear on the third day of the hermitage, as I can see from my diary: *I remain stranded when I have to hide my true nature, my inner core.*

Doing so brings about unpleasant scenes, as with Barbara this weekend.

I cannot be anyone but who I am.

Right, and I am not a man who is made for life with a woman.

Only now do I again clearly recognize what I have repressed from my consciousness for a long time: in response to the explicit, homosexual images of the third day, on day four, I heard clearly and understandably from the depth of my soul: »You need not be afraid of your sexuality. It is your direct path to the spiritual.«

That can only mean my homosexuality. It is closely connected to my need for spirituality. Although I still do not understand how to make a connection between them.

The girl who appeared to me in my dream does not prevent this interpretation. In her role as a seer, she recognizes my dilemma from her distant perspective and offers a way out.

I must take the initiative myself if I want to be free. If only I can free myself from my shackles. When I have found the courage to do so, then will I experience the world in all its breadth. It will open to me. To me. Not us.

Nowhere does the vision of a two-person relationship with a woman reveal itself to me. Therefore, there is no need to think along these lines any longer. Instead, I am free to do what I want. No monastery, no girlfriend, nobody tells me what to do. This is the truth: it is absolutely right that Barbara and I go our separate ways – it is an indication of authenticity, not of failure.

To have made so much progress on my path to recognition means a lot to me. The chapter ›Barbara‹ is now closed in my heart, too.

But what happens now? What awaits me next on my serpentine path? I cannot look beyond the next bend. Unfortunately. I may not know what to do, but I can rely on HIS plan.

A few days later, at my favorite newsstand, an esoteric magazine catches my eye that looks like it might hold some answers for me. At home, I leaf through the glossy pages in a hurry. My eyes jump restlessly over ads and event announcements. I only know what I am looking for when I see it. Electrified, I read the little message. The hairs on my arms stand up; pleasant goose bumps cover my body. What a coincidence! I can hardly believe it. I never thought I would have such a chance!

So, when is it?

I am so excited. My heart is racing, and my thoughts are in turmoil. I must study the few lines several times before I understand all the details, and a first plan emerges in my head. How wonderful that my work is only part-time. It should not be a problem to be away for a few days, even so soon. The date is nearly here already.

God will not let me fall. How right I was in choosing the theme for the invitations to my solemn profession: the protecting hand prevents the fall, gives security, and means trust in God. That is why I know that today – only a few weeks after intensive self-examination – I am right to be in Berlin. I am here to attend my first ›SkyDancing Tantra‹ workshop.

What an ambiance: the hall is festively decorated with exotic flowers, countless candles, and colorful fabrics. There is even a kind of altar, beautifully decorated, with power objects. There is an eye-catcher in the middle of the room: a futon veiled in an impressive Balinese fabric.

And there she is: Margot Anand – a French woman of Russian origin, bestselling author, founder of a Tantra Institute, and a Tantra instructor. What Adelindis knows, she learned from her. Margot is surrounded by a royal aura as she walks to the futon with only a sarong and sacral jewelry on her body. Yet, I can hardly take my eyes off her partner, Leonard: apart from a hat and extravagant jewelry, I especially like his silky shimmering sarong and his muscular, naked upper body.

The futon seems to be waiting just for this beautiful couple.

Music begins to play. Leonard rises and dances towards Margot. Following the fast rhythm of the music, her partner moves with virility. With great expression, he courts Margot, who becomes his love goddess, his Shakti. And she lets herself be carried away by the intoxicating energy of her love god, Shiva.

Softer melodic sounds also transform the heated atmosphere in the room. Now it is Shakti's turn to express her desire. Astonished, I watch how beautifully she enchants Shiva, putting her openness for a melting together into her graceful movements.

They meet at the futon, taking places opposite each other with their legs folded below them, sitting on their heels. Both close their eyes and breathe deeply through pursed lips. Their pelvises move back and forth, with their right hands, they trace their movements in front of their bodies. With a loud »Ahh« they breathe out.

First, they synchronize their breathing with eyes wide open until they begin to breathe in counter-rhythm – faster and faster, all the while their hands are mapping the rhythm in front of their bodies. Their noisy breathing turns into a growl, which increases to screeching mating sounds. They put their palms together, pressing them against each other more and more as if they were trying to resist each other. Shiva and Shakti have transformed into two powerful animals in courtship. Conquest and defense, resistance and possession. In a cacophony of shrill sounds, their desire explodes.

While the other participants in the power circle seem impressed, I am more reserved. I do not find my previous experience with Tantra reflected in this presentation. At least for now, it is difficult for me to categorize this extraordinary performance.

After this loud eruption, the mood is different: more loving, more tender. Shiva sits cross-legged. With his sarong slightly open, he invites Shakti to sit on his lap. Their bodies nestling up against each other, they breathe deeply in and out – first in sync, then in counter-rhythm – slowly increasing the tempo of their breathing – faster and faster, more and more violent, reaching an incredible intensity – and then an abrupt stop. The ensuing silence is complete.

What a furious ending. I could not have wished for a more exciting conclusion to these last three days than to be part of the ›Wave of Bliss.‹ At least as a spectator. I would only really learn it if I booked the annual seminar ›Training in Love and

Ecstasy.‹ But in my mind, I can already see myself closely entwined as the hero of this erotic scene. And the image does not feel strange, has nothing odd about it. Instead, it seems merely to anticipate the next step in my development, as if my life were saying to me: YES! Your destiny is fulfilled here, in this tantric world in which the divine spark ignites sexuality. I want more of that, to learn more, to understand better that which still seems mysterious, and above all, to try out for myself what I have just seen.

First, however, free dancing has been planned; expressive meditations and partner exercises in which distance, closeness, and touch are practiced. Much is said about ›sexual alchemy.‹ Despite these manifold, sometimes confusing impressions, on the third and last day of my trip in this new world, a great YES! echoes within me.

It is only when, on the train ride home, I make a sketchy note of the stirring experiences and their significance for my future life begins to emerge that I realize how I was also captivated by the incredible, powerful silence with which the ›wave of bliss‹ broke so abruptly. Why?

I am familiar with this silence. It became my confidante during my last years in the monastery when I did not know up from down. I sought it in the heart prayer or in silent meditation. Now I encounter it again here in Berlin – in completely different circumstances of life and meaning. Once again, it provides a counterpoint to the everyday.

YES! If that is not a sign, I do not know what is.

The iconic lights on the Berlin Europa Center had earlier seemed to me like a symbol for a hidden energy channel. In their alternation of ascending and descending sequence, do the flashing lamps not depict the flow of sexual and spiritual energy from the pelvis to the head and vice versa?

»YES!«

Entirely imbued with tantric energy, I saw the ›Breathing the Inner Flute‹ very clearly in this colorful picture.

Knowing that I would never have been able to get over it had financial hurdles prevented me from realizing my life's dream, I am grateful that Margot is willing to accommodate me regarding the course fees for the upcoming year-long training. She must sense how I have become fascinated by the tantric world and wants to help me explore.

Ten days of the first training session begin the day after Christmas in 1990. While my former monastic brothers sing songs about the holy birth of Christ in the Christmas Octave, I spend an extremely enjoyable time with twenty men and twenty women, couples, and singles in a seminar hotel at Chiemsee. We dance, laugh, meditate and get to know each other. With my unusual biography as a former monk, I am the undisputed center of interest.

The ›Dynamic Streaming Process‹ on the third day is a particularly formative experience. Margot promises that whole-body orgasms will be triggered exclusively through deep massage. And she is right. My exercise partner's devoted tissue stimulation creates deep vibrations in my body from the lower legs up the knees and pelvis and continues in waves in the upper body, neck, and head. Even my hands and arms are caught in this intoxication and tremble in utmost excitement. Through deep breaths, I multiply the feelings of lust many times over until I reach a heavenly level.

I need the privacy of my hotel room to understand what has happened: Through this great exercise, my world of perception has expanded in a wonderful way.

My icon of Mary, which travels with me, is close by as I immerse myself in the silence of meditation in order to contain the over-excitement that has been triggered. Although the elation carried me over every boundary, I came back down to earth only moments later. I am still unable to deal with overstimulation. Again and again, the inner pain sets in too quickly, forcing me to withdraw from the world. I am glad that Margot knows something about my story. The years of monastic life and the turning away from the world for so many hours of meditation have shaped me and left their traces. In this, I am in my profound spiritual experiences ahead of the other participants.

»Armin, I really don't understand how you, seen from the outside, had the most joyful, happy, and ecstatic experience in this room when you lived in the monastery a celibate life for ten years.«

Yes, and no.

Yes, I hear Margot's words in the sharing session the day after this surprisingly deep experience.

No. I do not understand what she is talking about or what she is trying to say.

Is it not good and wonderful that I feel so much freedom in my sexuality?

»Oh.«

That is all I can say. All eyes are upon me. I feel uncomfortable. I slide restlessly on my seat cushion.

»I do not understand how lust and celibacy go together!«

Margot's tone of voice puzzles me. I never heard her like that before.

»Yes,« I reply reluctantly.

What does that mean? I am at a loss for words and somehow out of my depth. My euphoria of the day before is gone. Embarrassed, I lower my eyes. I do not know what to say. Am I supposed to justify my life story?

Silence descends over the group.

»Thank you, Armin.«

The chance to explain myself is gone. The participant sitting next to me is already talking very vividly about her »fabulous climax« of the day before and receives nods and approving murmurs from the others as well as a benevolent comment from Margot. Here, appreciation resonates.

I am getting annoyed with myself. At the decisive moment, I remained as mute as a fish. I wish I had been able to take a stand.

Who among those present is better prepared for an encounter with God in the tantric union than I am? I am one of the very few participants who devoted themselves very intensively to spiritual teachings. I have spent years on the hesychastic path. Even more time on the seat cushion immersed in Christian Zen meditation, meeting my sense of pleasure spiritually. That is why I have long been able to give sexual energy a direction other than that of discharge. What the others learn only in this course has been a daily practice for me since my encounter with Amatus.

So it is more than strange to hear from Margot's words that I lack deeper insight into the real connections.

Or am I simply reacting over sensitively because my

spiritual teachers have given me urgent warnings before? Indeed, to not delve deeper into such matters, least of all to confront myself with them: »Don't get any ideas! Don't hang your ego on it!« Like a soundtrack, Father Anton's words still ring in my ears.

Now, however, I am supposed to discuss this spiritual miracle with several dozen strangers. Here this mysterious energy event becomes the center of interest, nothing less. That is why we are here.

Nevertheless, I was not able to express the right words today. For me, it makes a difference whether I visit a retreat with Lejonidas or training with Margot. I have not yet found my place in her circle.

Even here, however, I am mistaken: »We choose you, dear Armin.«

With outstretched hands and bright eyes, Leonard steps up to me as if to take me in his arms. I feel seen, truly chosen, and destined for greater things.

»The tarot cards have revealed to Margot and I that of all the participants, you have the greatest integrative power. You are destined to be the first to undergo the healing ritual today. Are you ready for the awakening of your ecstatic potential?«

I am mesmerized by Leonard's beautifully curving lips.

I nod without a word.

»Would you care to demonstrate the exercise with me?«

I am nearly ready to believe that another dream is about to come true. What a way to start the New Year. Of course, I agree.

I am permitted to add one item to our ritual taking place on the futon in the middle of the circle. Naturally, I turn to my trusted icon of Mary, the keeper of my soul. I place her next to the mat so that I have my unique power object firmly in view.

Leonard and I begin the exercise with a ›heart-to-heart greeting.‹ Warmth, calmness, and friendliness come toward me. My heart opens. At the climax of the ritual, my whole body shivers.

Then suddenly, I feel an inexplicable blockage as my gaze falls on my faithful icon of Mary as if she was suddenly standing in my way instead of accompanying me. Searching for help, I look to Leonard. Then, again, at the picture of the Virgin Mary. Unable to speak, I point with a trembling hand at Margot, who is sitting far away from me at the very end of the room.

»You want Margot to come here,« Leonard asks sensitively. I nod and am glad when the icon disappears from my view. Helpful spirits have conjured it away.

It is obvious that its power has ceased to work.

As Margot hesitantly approaches, she seems to me more than a kind, caring mother. At this moment, I recognize her as the guardian of the road ahead of me, as if she has been sent to me by Providence. She is the female person to whom I must entrust myself in order to be led into sexual freedom. She has the knowledge that will help me to direct lust and desire in completely new ways. Far away from old, well-known doctrines. I cannot get any closer to my ideal of the fusion of spirituality and sexuality. I am experiencing pure bliss.

It is wonderful that I am able to share this revelation with the other participants. The whole group congratulates me on my extraordinary insight. The apparent discord of the second day has been overshadowed.

I return home again on January 5th, enthusiastic. I think back not only to the spectacular worlds of experience but also to the ›house game‹ assignments that I have received: to practice, practice, practice what we have learned. Like Adelindis, I have been officially commissioned by Margot to enrich the world with tantric energy.

The question is only which world is meant: mine or the other. There are serious differences between them. In Margot's world, Shiva meets Shakti. In her course, I experience this divine act of creation. Perhaps in this way, I still fulfill some subliminal longing for heterosexual life.

Yet in my private life, I want to have freedom of expression to remain true to my preferences. An authentic life in which I take the liberty of questioning the given: Why should the divine only show itself in heterosexuality? As Margot's messenger, even missionary, am I not commissioned to bring divine energy to remote corners of the world, for example, to the gay subculture? That is where my journey must go. Only then does Margot's missionary assignment make sense to me.

Since it seems there is nothing more important now than to follow my intuition, I visit sauna clubs, flirt at hot parties, and start to learn my way around Birkensee Lake.

I do not yet know how things are going for the others, but I am already looking forward to their reactions when I report in the large circle on how eagerly I completed my ›house games.‹

In June, I return to the embrace of my Tantra family. We start the second training with a round of sharing. Most of them talk about ›sex in unusual locations.‹ Some announce separations, and two men are happy about new romantic relationships. I can hardly wait my turn.

Exuberant, I start with a toast to my safety bag: »Right up front, I can say: the safety bag was a big hit! Nobody was as well-equipped as I was. Of course, condoms and lubricants are not exactly the biggest attraction. But knowing how to use massage oil and aromatic essences makes all the difference, I can tell you.«

The silence in the room further encourages me to revel in my memories. »I always had these with me when I was cruising at Birkensee, of course! For those who don't know it well, I'll briefly describe what it's like there.«

I see eyes open wide. Many participants have their mouths open; breathless tension even seems to have taken hold of Margot and Leonard.

»Naked men are scattered in the forest or stroll along the trampled paths. Their restlessness is palpable as they search for their prey. I did it more subtly: on the prowl, I connect with my breath, feeling step by step the touching and rolling of the soles of my feet. As if it were the most natural thing in the world, I practice being present, like I learned in Zen meditation. Of course, I would never have suspected that one-day meditative walking would lead me to successful cruising. But that's just the way it is: you can do meditation everywhere.«

Excited about the feedback from the attendees, I finish my summary.

The room is so quiet we could have heard a pin drop. The longer the silence lasts, the more the tension increases: have I gone too far? Was I too explicit in my description of homosexual subculture? Will I hear a rebuke in Margot's words again?

»Yes, Armin, these are your experiences,« Margot says after some time.

»You have realized that Tantra has nothing to do with sexual orientation. Tantra transcends it. And you are welcome to continue with us as you are!«

Yes! What an accolade. I am so moved I do not know what to say, so I just nod modestly.

Inside, however, I feel strongly moved. As a good mother does, she has just given me the blessing to follow my sexual orientation like an inner compass on my educational journey through the world of Tantra, as Margot teaches it.

And with it, old dogmas have suddenly lost their validity. Sexuality is not bad. Homosexuality is by no means doubly bad. It must be understood correctly: The sexual act, as practiced in Tantra, leads to spiritual enlightenment. Margot has confirmed that same-sex sex is not excluded. If sexuality is not an end in itself but a possible way to connect to an experience of God, then I may go this way. Even with men.

What a magnificent outlook! I know already that this training session will not offer a major triumph over my inner conflict.

Is that also true of my new civilian life? How is my self-confidence? Will my free-spirited ideas be just as controversial in the Caritas Pirckheimer House as they were at Metten? Can I not already see the signs of disaster now?

»So, what are you actually studying in your courses?«

This direct question hits a nerve and immediately transports me to the last phase of my days in Metten. I did not expect to be asked »for a word« with the CPH team leader, finding myself in a situation that reminds me of the many intense conversations in Abbot Berthold's office.

Like then, I try to disavow any guilty behavior, but I do not forget that my point of view is not always shared. With unpleasant consequences.

»What do you mean?« I ask unsuspectingly.

»I have heard some nice things about you!« As if he could not believe it, he repeats: »Good things!«

What is that supposed to mean? Do I have reason to be concerned? Has someone complained about me? Dark thoughts haunt my mind as I try to figure out what to say under the unwavering gaze of my interlocutor.

Did I once again take too much liberty and underestimate the institutional ways? I feel both hot and cold at the thought of not having learned my lesson, of having fallen into the same trap as in Metten. Is the past really going to repeat itself here? Is it even possible? Am I not someone and somewhere else in my new life?

»Mr. Heining? Did you hear me?«

The team leader's voice sounds as friendly as ever.

»Yes, of course. I'm pleased that the response to my approach is so positive that you hear many nice things.«

»I've heard stories about massages – and I couldn't believe it.«

He leans over the desk and slaps it with the palm of his hand.

»Massages!« he shouts.

»Phenomenal! We've never had that here before. What a great idea!«

Nearly exploding, he bursts out into thunderous laughter.

»Whatever gave you that idea? I have to hear it from you in person.«

»I simply want to bring more of my personal experience to my work. Organizing school days for students of different grades from Franconia is only one aspect. The exciting part is the work in small groups on the topics of their choice, the interactive church services, game evenings, and so on. But I thought that even more could be achieved – especially considering my monastic experience and my knowledge of different immersion techniques.«

»These are particularly important qualifications that you

mention. You have a broad spectrum of religious and spiritual understanding.« Mr. Lindemann nods approvingly.

Thus strengthened, I am happy to go on. My uncertainty has disappeared. I feel myself on safe ground.

»I have been attending a Tantra course in my spare time for several months now, taught by Margot Anand, the founder of the SkyDancing Institute. She attaches great importance to teaching us the practice of mindfulness. And I thought it would be a good idea to break down appropriate rituals to a place of encounter where teenagers can learn to treat each other with respect. Doing good for each other, giving comforting gifts like a hand or foot massage, promotes trust and directs the focus away from over-stimulation, permanent consumption, and self-centeredness.«

Did Mr. Lindemann flinch at the mention of ›Tantra?‹ Maybe, but my success clearly proves me right; he just admitted it.

As if he were hard of hearing, he leans over the table again, turning his right ear to me.

»Where did you say your ideas came from?«

»SkyDancing Tantra. In my spare time, I attend seminars.«

»So, I see.«

He leans back again, his head low. »Well, that name... that name is something very off the ground.«

He pauses.

»So be it. Those exercises you're teaching are worth their weight in gold. Keep it up! Keep it up.«

What remarkable praise. I did not always make friends with my openness and unconventionality during my time in Metten. There, these qualities drove me into isolation.

Here I am able to take the opportunity to be recognized. I very much hope that public opinion does not change. After all, I am employed by a Catholic institution, and the principles of the Catholic Church are immutable.

»There is one more thing you should perhaps know...« I start and pause for a moment.

»Yes, Mr. Heining?«

His inquisitive gaze feels encouraging.

»I am the only... homosexual student at SkyDancing.«

Need I say more?

Amazingly, my team leader does not appear surprised.

»Nothing human is strange to me, Mr. Heining. You can count on my understanding. That's fine.«

With a sympathetic nod, I am free to go. I really am on a roll. Who could have seen this coming?

I have not forgotten the lesson of my time in Würzburg: if I show myself as I really am, friendships break. Albin,

Clemens, and Humbert did not want to connect with my inner place at that time and the consequences it imposed on me. Today I am happy not to have relied on their supposed friendship but to have taken to heart the advice of the wise Father Claudius: »Find out what interests you; what inclination do you want to investigate? What do you need to realize your potential?«

Nonetheless, I have not forgotten my despair at that time about the pain of my inner turmoil; the break between my inner and outer self was simply too severe. Only during tantric union does the separation of body, mind, and soul cease to exist at all. What was separated is reunited. I again belong to myself completely – as a healed self, as soon as I have crossed the threshold between spirituality and sexuality.

I think back to the cover of the book that Abbot Gabriel once presented to me: two golden deities intimately united, fused into a perfect union. That must have been the beginning of all being before every formative experience that made its mark on my world. In ›tantric union‹ there is no trace of worldly toil or earthly laws.

I am carried up to this highest level of enlightenment by the ›wave of bliss.‹ Triggered by rhythmic breathing and tension of the pelvic floor muscles, its powerful dynamics lift me to the last stage of my path of transformation. Here I get a glimpse of the cosmic dimension of all beings. I grasp the structure of my world and recognize the divine plan: I see it in the interplay of all forces until the great wave ebbs away with a wafer-thin ripple of gently electrifying tension. This is the undeniable highlight of the third and last module of Margot's year-long training program.

Which I wish I could maintain in my daily life. The sad truth is: I do not know what I will do when it is over. Without regularly spending time with my Tantra family, I am threatened by a truly dark void after the bright highlights of the last few months – when Margot will no longer offer me maternal advice.

I have no other choice than to talk to her now. Leonard listens as I try to put my anguish into words.

»For me, the end of the training is connected with great pain: With you and the others, I have experienced respect and appreciation in being together, learned so much in communicating about physicality and sensuality, not to mention the intoxicating fusion of sexuality and spirituality.«

»It's hard for us to say goodbye every time, too. Nevertheless, we are happy about the positive experiences you will take with you,« Margot says.

»I believe you. Unfortunately, the reality of life in the gay scene is completely different. Ephemeral, casual sex, gossip, mean words. No sense of mindfulness!«

Margot and Leonard look at each other.

Perhaps they do not want such an intimate look behind the scenes. I cannot worry about that now. I need to get what is bothering me off my chest.

»Of course, I find the non-commitment of sexual encounters exciting; a partnership is not the model for my life. It's just a pity that I can't find a place in the whole gay scene where I feel comfortable. Such a home, however, would be that much more important for me since I have come to the conclusion that my homosexuality is not a blemish that clings to my ego or even overshadows my life but rather that it is an orientation that I am willing to follow.«

Again, they look at each other.

»Do you know what I mean? Where do I go from here? Where will my journey take me in the future? How am I supposed to be able to apply what I have learned here in my everyday life when most gay men don't seem to be ready to add spirituality to their sex lives?«

I pause; the sense of hopelessness threatens to overwhelm me: »I can't imagine what my life will be like without ...«

My voice breaks.

They both remain respectfully silent, yet I feel completely understood. More than ever, I see Margot as an understanding mother who supports me with advice and action even in difficult phases.

»I have only just found what I have longed for all my life, and now it appears to have been only a fleeting episode?«

»The local groups have given you strength, haven't they?« Leonard says.

»Yes, tremendous. Outside the courses, this has always been a wonderful port on the Tantric River. But they are also over,« I sadly conclude.

»And what about friendships? Has nothing resulted from the contacts you were able to make here? We always had the impression that you integrated very well. Isn't that right?«

»Yes, that's right,« Margot agrees, to my great delight.

»We exchanged phone numbers, but out of sight, out of mind, as they say. No friendships have developed further. That's why I'm at such a loss.«

Both are silent. Having stated my case, I, too, have nothing more to say. Now I hope for their bright ideas.

Finally, Leonard sighs from the depth of his heart: »Dear Armin. If there is no such room in which you can feel comfortable and authentic with your lust, with your love, with your sexuality and spirituality, you must create it for yourself.«

»Create it yourself?« I echo.

»Yes. Create your own Tantric heaven. Our SkyDancing instructor training might be just what you need. You could learn the basics there.«

I look at Margot in disbelief. She nods, a friendly smile on her lips. So, this suggestion is to be taken seriously.

This is a fascinating idea – no question about it. Especially since I had already imagined in my small quiet apartment what it would be like to organize Tantra evenings myself. Do I not also have – thanks to my spiritual background – the inner competence to pass on Margot's teachings? In my bold dreams, I succeed in creating an atmosphere in which men, in particular, can experience their spiritual awakening safely and securely, where outer intimacy and inner truth are shared without pressure to perform and without potential for conflict, but with respect and deep love.

I would emphasize shared breathing exercises because they multiply sexual and sensory tensions until they never unleash before experienced ecstasy. I can already see how the respectful spirit of the group connects complete strangers and inspires them to go on a wonderful journey of discovery together.

Yes, this could be my life. If I did not already have a job and a single profession but several.

I am not only a qualified theologian but will soon complete my training as a pastoral adviser; at the same time, my training year for educators will end – after twenty-four instead of twelve months. Because I do not work full-time, the rule is: half a job, double the training year.

My civilian life is so solid and resistant to crises. With the passing of the Second Service Examination, a number of doors will be open to me in the Catholic world – even as a lay theologian. That I may assume the position of pastoral adviser for life is assured.

That this is indeed the case is proven by a letter that reaches me out of the blue and forces me to make a decision. In a polite, albeit clear letter, I hope to strike the right note without going into too much detail:

Unfortunately, I will not grant your request for an application. Personal reasons are what motivate me to do so: After a religious education and close affiliation with the Church (monk and deacon in the Benedictine Abbey of Metten/Lower Bavaria from 1980 to 1990), it seems to me to be more important for my life's development to distance myself a little more from the Catholic Church. Therefore, I plan to become more engaged in freelance seminar work and guidance. Perhaps there will be the possibility to collaborate in this way.

I cannot foresee the effect of my words, however.

»I spoke up for you, expressly recommending you to the Episcopal Academy because I was pleased with your success in training and want to offer you a future under our roof.«

The director of the CPH is somewhat annoyed.

»Your refusal is surprising. What's stopping you from applying for this job?«

Now his face is red, and his expression is darkening.

I had not expected such a strong reaction from Father Huber. Still, I am firmly convinced that I reacted appropriately. Perhaps it is just a misunderstanding.

»Of course, I appreciate that you consider me suitable to fill the position of lecturer for practical, cultural work and extra-occupational education in connection with the management of a conference institution. For this reason, I am extremely pleased that you are giving me the opportunity to thank you personally once again today for your intercession, Father Huber. I am honored that you have such a high opinion of me.«

My carefully chosen words have the right effect. The director seems to be appeased already; I even see a little smile at the corners of his mouth.

»This makes it all the more difficult for me not to apply.«

Before the next sentence, I pause to take a deep breath.

»Director, I have come to realize that I identify as homosexual. At such a prominent place in the Catholic Church, I would not be able to live my orientation openly. And I am not willing to lead a double life.«

Father Huber's face darkens; he conceals himself in a frosty silence that weighs on me the longer it lasts. I am forced to consider too many possible interpretations. Which one is plausible? Did my openness overwhelm him? Is homosexuality a problem for him? Have I misjudged him?

»I understand you.«

Just three simple words, but they mean the world to me. I had not been expecting understanding. Now I feel relieved that I was wrong. Unfortunately, the joyful surprise tightens my throat – I cannot speak.

»Yes, Mr. Heining, if that is the case, I can understand why you could not react differently. A guaranteed life has no value if the heart is not allowed to be there.«

Touched deeply and still mute, I merely nod. But when I take my leave, I take the Jesuit priest's outstretched hand.

»Mr. Heining, I wish you the best for your promising future.«

I have really changed! I note proudly in my diary on July 9th, 1992. Seized by an overwhelming feeling of great astonishment, I write down my most important thoughts at home: *I still can hardly believe how I actually succeeded in confronting a man of the church with a taboo subject and still got respect and recognition. Probably because I simply let the official church keep its conviction while I go my way without criticizing it, without regard to the consequences. I will*

Since I began practicing Tantra regularly, my life is no longer full of contradictions. There are no longer oppositions piling up on top of each other that demand my attention and need to be overcome.

Since I no longer see a fundamental contradiction in my life – the incompatibility of homosexuality with an experience of God – and since I live my sexuality as a divinely inspired spiritual experience, my whole life has changed.

It is as if I can see what is really going on in the glow of the Tabor Light of divine knowledge. There is no ugly shadow that takes the light away from me. There is only one life free from deception.

Abbot Berthold comes to my mind. I wonder how he would react if he knew how much I owe him.

Although my actions, by the standards he set, left him no choice, the key message of the memorable February talks was not only: »We don't want to let you fall.«

I believe there was another message that I was unable to grasp at the time: ›I have reached the position of deacon, but climbing another rung on this ladder is not possible now. Life in the Benedictine monastery and priesthood are not my way forward. It is not for me to live in the vessel of the Catholic Church.‹

Despite the circumstances, he always supported me and took care of me; out of nowhere, this examination year suddenly appeared and gave me undreamed-of opportunities that I was ready to use. My freedom today took its roots here.

I dared to engage in a particularly deep form of active meditation: Tantra. Even when the people around silent meditation always warned me against it, calling it a pure illusion of a spiritual path.

»Is she credible to you, that is, coherent?« Lejonidas asked me frankly one day. I recognized in Margot the enlightened Shakti. Not him. On the contrary, in modern Tantra, even unconventional practice leads to enlightenment.

Margot understands that the divine guidance of the soul can also be experienced while cruising at the lake. She strengthened my belief that spirituality does not cease to exist in homosexual lust. Access to immanent transcendence, to the divine within me, which I have been searching for since my childhood, is not denied to me by my homosexuality.

On the contrary, only in the sexual act – celebrated in tantric ritual – is the heavenly act of creation reinterpreted. Humans themselves become deities in whose bodies the universe is reflected. In this higher reality, there is no difference between the earthly and the divine.

Here there is only the true core of my being, to which I was allowed to return.

Epilogue

December 28th, 1993.

I overlook everything; dark green pine forests, snow-covered mountains, and crystal clear streams lie miles below me and stretch as far as the eye can see to the end of my world. And there is something else: a small orange house with a yellow roof. There is a lot of activity around it – all men.

Just above me, a bright blue sky, so close you can touch it. Even the sun shines within reach. My world is beautiful.

Until the first clouds appear, curling around my forehead and finally obscuring my view. The cool wind makes me shiver. It is high time to leave.

But where to? And how? A queasy feeling creeps over me as I look down: There is nearly nothing beneath me. I can just about sense the first spiral that extends to a widening base.

But I am not there. I am standing on the highest and smallest point of this spiraling snail shell – and I am about to lose my balance. It is completely impossible to remain up here on this pin-sized tip. I have no foothold or safe ground. There is no safety net to catch my fall, of that I am sure.

Dark clouds are approaching; thunder is rumbling in the distance, and a squall is driving me into the depths. ›Pride comes before a fall‹ is my last thought.

www.ingramcontent.com/pod-product-compliance
Lightning Source LLC
Chambersburg PA
CBHW051552030726
47592CB00001B/245